W9-BRO-119

CHILDREN'S LITERARY HOUSES

FAMOUS DWELLINGS IN CHILDREN'S FICTION

CHILDREN'S LITERARY HOUSES

FAMOUS DWELLINGS IN CHILDREN'S FICTION

ROSALIND ASHE AND LISA TUTTLE
RESEARCHED BY
TALIA RODGERS

Facts On File Publications
New York, New York • Bicester, England

First published in the United States of America by
Facts On File, Inc., 460 Park Avenue South, New York, NY 10016.

First published in the United Kingdom by Dragon's World Limited.

Library of Congress Cataloging in Publication Data.

Ashe, Rosalind.
Children's Literary Houses.

Summary: Describes and provides illustrations, maps, and plans of eight famous fictional houses featured in "David Copperfield", "Little Women", "Robinson Crusoe", "Alice in Wonderland", "Charlotte's Web" and other classic stories.

1. Children's stories, English – Stories, plots, etc.
2. Children's stories, American – Stories, plots, etc.
3. Setting (Literature). 4. Dwellings in literature.
5. Architecture, Domestic, in literature. [1. English fiction – Stories, plots, etc. 2. American fiction – Stories, plots, etc. 3. Dwellings – Fiction.
4. Architecture, Domestic – Fiction] I. Tuttle, Lisa, 1952- . II. Title. III. Title: Literary houses.
PR830.S48A78 1984 823'.0872'09 84-10143
ISBN 0-87196-971-8.

Printed in Germany

Acknowledgement is due to: The Watkins Lumis Agency, New York, for permission to reprint from THE SECRET GARDEN by Frances Hodgson Burnett; to William Collins Sons and Co. Ltd and Putnams for permission to reprint from THE SWORD IN THE STONE. © Copyright T. H. White, published by Collins; to Hamish Hamilton Ltd. London, and Harper and Row Inc. New York, for permission to reprint from CHARLOTTE'S WEB by E. B. White; and to The Marie Rodell-Frances Collin Agency, New York, for permission to reprint from JOHNNY TREMAIN by Esther Forbes.

FOREWORD

A book is like a house. It is only after you open the cover, or open the door, that you discover what it is really like. Venturing further in, you can sense the atmosphere, and learn from the rooms and how they are furnished something of the people who live there. You may even wonder what it would be like to live there yourself.

Houses, especially houses in fiction, are more than bricks and mortar, more than boards and beams, more than just a frame for the events that take place within them. It isn't Colin or Mary or Dickon that readers of *The Secret Garden* most want to meet, it's Misselthwaite Manor, marooned on the moors, and the garden itself, abandoned for years behind high, ivy-clad walls.

Not all the houses we explore here are actually *houses* — as well as the March family's comfortable home, here is a beached boat, a fortified stockade on a deserted island, and a cosy, sweet smelling barn. Here also is an eighteenth century Boston silversmith's shop, a vast, lonely manor house, and a medieval castle.

What all these very different dwellings do have in common is that they all come from classic stories which have appealed to many readers, over many years — and they are all fantastic places to explore.

The words and pictures here have been put together from clues gleaned from the author's original text, with additional research into period decoration, architecture, gardens, boatbuilding, weaponry and furniture. As well as aiming for accuracy in details (what sort of tools did a silversmith use in a pre-Revolutionary Boston?) we have tried to capture some of the flavour of each book, a little of the magic which has made these literary houses seem so real.

So, turn the page. Open a door.

CONTENTS

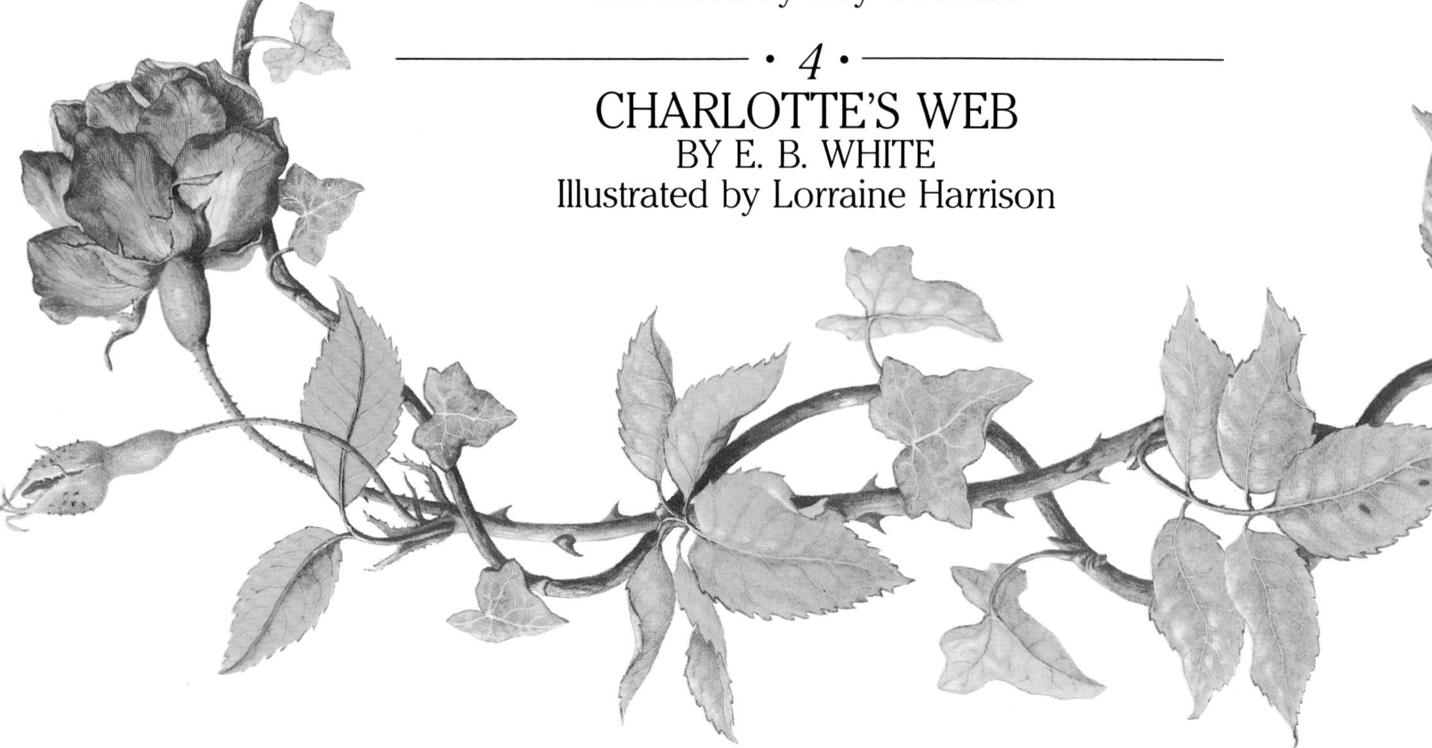

THE SECRET GARDEN

"It was the sweetest, most mysterious-looking place anyone could imagine. The high walls which shut it in were covered with the leafless stems of climbing roses, which were so thick they were matted together . . . It was this hazy tangle from tree to tree which made it look so mysterious."

I don't like this house. It's spooky and full of mysteries. What is behind the hundred closed doors along the winding corridors? What is it that cries in the night? They said it was just the wind. Why is my guardian so strangely sad, so much of the time away? Why does he seem to

hate this place? Where is the hidden garden that Martha has told me of? How can you shut up a garden, lock it away and bury the key?

It was night when I came to Misselthwaite Manor, and I do not recall much of the journey here, except for the smart carriage with a footman that met us at the station; and I remember looking out into the darkness as we travelled and seeing a great black sea: "that is the Moor", said Mrs Medlock. There was an avenue of bare trees like a vault, and at last the house, so long and low, with one solitary window lighted, and the solemn door opening. The butler said, "The Master does not want to see the child now, and is going away in the morning." I felt like a small black beetle lost in the great hall. Nobody wanted me, an orphan of ten, still in mourning. But this was to be my new home.

Today, Mr Craven, my uncle-guardian, has sent me a writing case. And I have met him; he is sad and distant but quite kind. I have written to thank him and now I am going to set down my adventures here. The writing case has my initials on it in gold.

The first morning is quite clear to me: waking in the big strange room (I am used to it now), with dark tapestries of a forest and people in fancy-dress, and dogs and horses. Through the window I saw the moors again, dismal and purplish, going on for ever and not a tree in sight — not one bit like India, the only place I know. And there was only a maid clearing the grate; no ayah to dress me — and this girl seemed surprised I expected her to! She rattled on in a most unservantlike but friendly manner about her swarm of little brothers and sisters, especially "Dickon" who tamed a wild moor-pony for himself and "had a way with animals". I could not help being interested; and she wanted me to tell her about the elephants and wild boars in India.

The nursery next door had dark pictures and big dark furniture, not a bit like a real nursery — have they never had children in this house? — and a view of the gardens, with flowerbeds and trees; but all grey and dead.

Martha the maid gave me warm clothes and showed me the way into the grounds. It was she who told me that Mr Craven had locked up his favourite garden ten years ago when his young wife died. I walked along the paths to an old grey fountain; but there were no flowers, and the fountain had no water. There was a long walk beside a high wall covered in ivy. I went through a green door

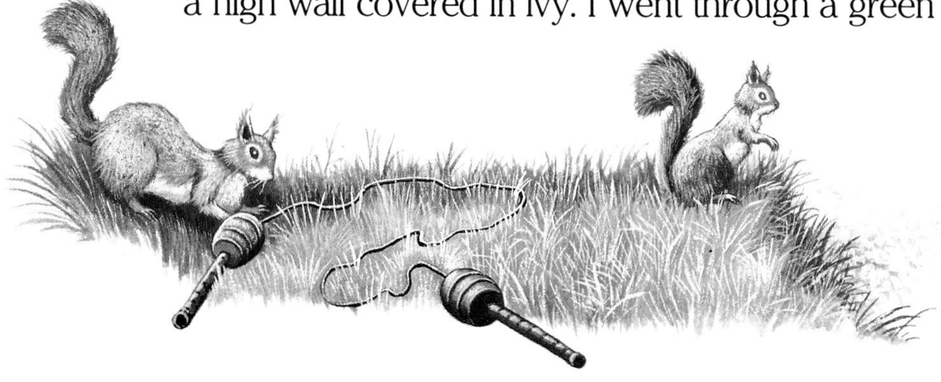

THE WOODS
WHERE MARY FIRST MET DICKON
THE SECRET GARDEN
X WHERE THE KEY WAS FOUND
ORCHARD
KITCHEN GARDENS
LONG WALK
ROSE BED
BENCHES
FLOWER BEDS
SHED
NURSERY BEDS
GREENHOUSE
STATUE
WALL OF SHRUBBERY
GATE
FORMAL
GARDENS
FOUNTAIN
FLOWER BEDS
LAWN
CLIPPED TREES
STABLES
RHODODENDRON BUSHES
RHODODENDRON WALK
SUNDIAL
ROSE TREES
TO THE
MISSELTHWAITE MANOR

and inside were glass frames and wintery vegetables, I think: very knobbly and ugly; and stiff black trees like iron candlesticks against the walls. A cross old man with a spade said there were only more gardens like that beyond the walls, and an orchard. I went on exploring; and then I met the little bird with his bright red chest: the only spot of colour alive in all that dead place. He *must* know about the hidden garden, I thought; what would it be like after ten years shut away? It must be the deadest garden of all.

The red bird whistled so cheerfully. (I remembered that boy Dickon: *he* would have known how to talk to it). Even the cross old gardener was nice when it flew down. It was a robin, he told me, and he knew it well; he said it liked me! — even though I was, like himself, "not much to look at", and "sour-faced"! Yorkshire people don't seem at all in awe of their betters as Indian servants are. I asked him about the hidden garden; but he said it had no door, and you can't get in.

Since then I often explore the garden. I was lonely; it was something to do. Martha brought me a skipping rope, so now I skip along the paths, and the robin keeps me company. I have been watching where he flies, but however round and about I go, I cannot get to his favourite tree on the other side of the wall. I believe that tree is standing in the secret garden.

The weather has been bad so I have been exploring the house instead. I am supposed to stay in my two big rooms, but no-one will know if I venture out quietly: nobody comes up except to bring me my meals; even Martha, who sometimes stays and talks to me about Dickon, is too busy during the day. I asked her about the crying I heard in the night but she said it was only the wind, and I could tell she was lying; and I've heard it again when there was no wind.

The house is very old and the corridors are full of corners and steps up and down and gloomy staircases. My favourite room looked like a lady's sitting room. It had embroidered velvet on the walls and a tall cabinet where I found rows and rows of ivory elephants all different sizes. I played with those; then I heard a rustling noise. I was quite surprised to find I was not the only live creature in the house: there was a mouse peeping from a cushion on the sofa! And creeping close I saw a whole family that had made their nest there!

I lost count of all the rooms I explored, and mistook my way so often I had to look out of the windows to discover which side I was. It was so silent and deserted — then I heard that crying sound again. I found a new corridor and a door hidden behind a tapestry. Then suddenly there was Mrs Medlock rattling her keys.

Never mind: I have uncovered one great secret in the garden — the robin helped me. And I have met Dickon at last, and he is in on my secret. I shall solve this mystery too, and no-one can stop me, so there!

What a strange house! One hundred closed rooms, a locked-up garden, and now a shut-away boy!

In the dead of night I followed the crying sound and found him. He thought I was a ghost. He is called Colin. He is Mr Craven's son — my cousin! — and he is a bedridden invalid. Neither of us knew about one another

all this time. He is kept shut away for a terrible reason: his mother died when he was born, and his father cannot bear to see him, since the poor boy looks so like her. I heard the tale from Colin himself, and more today from Martha who helps look after him but like everyone else is sworn to secrecy. Colin certainly looks sickly; his father and the doctor fear he is going to be a hunchback — and my cousin is quite terrified; they all want him to die, he says, and so does he. But I think he is mostly lonely and weak from lack of exercise (exercise has made *me* strong: even my hair is thicker!) He has a fierce temper and behaves very haughtily and rudely to the servants, like a young rajah shut up in that grand room. He seems to like me and wants me to go back.

Now I find that Dickon knew about him too — I was the only one in the dark! Dickon comes pretty well every day now Spring is nearly here, and we work away together at our great secret. I have never seen Spring before: it is Magic, like Dickon with his animals. I have told Colin about Dickon and how he understands creatures and growing things - though I dared

not tell him our secret for fear he might blurt it out in one of his tantrums. Although he hates people looking at him, he wants to see Dickon.

And today Dickon came up to visit him, with Captain the fox cub, Soot the raven, his two tame squirrels Nut and Shell, and a new-born lamb he had found on the moor beside its dead mother. Already Colin looks better, and has stopped saying he wants to die. Dickon and I are hatching a plan. When the weather gets warmer . . .

We have told Colin our secret.

I suppose I had talked so often of the mystery of the garden with no door: he loved to hear about it and what it would be like *if* we found a way in . . .

The robin showed me the way. He helped me find the buried key — so I knew there must be a door. Many days I hunted for it; and then one blustery winter's morning the wind blew the ivy aside, and I saw it. Colin listened wide-eyed as I told him how at last I entered the secret garden, so silent and dead and hung about with sad grey garlands of bare briars looped from tree to tree — more like the ghost of a garden. Then how I noticed little green points in the earth, and I started clearing away the rough grasses and weeds to help them come through. When I met Dickon it was even better: I knew he was skilled at making things grow, and I felt that if he could keep secrets about birds' nests and foxes' holes he would keep mine. So I showed him. He was as excited about it as I; and together we weeded and dug and pruned there — all unbeknownst to anyone else — and looked forward to the Spring. The snowdrops came first, then the crocuses; and it *was* like magic: a little crack where a whole new world was about to open and transform that shut, forsaken wilderness. Dickon showed me the roses were not dead; now, I told Colin, they are putting out tender pink shoots, and the daffodills are like bundles of sun.

We are going to take him out in a wheel-chair to see it

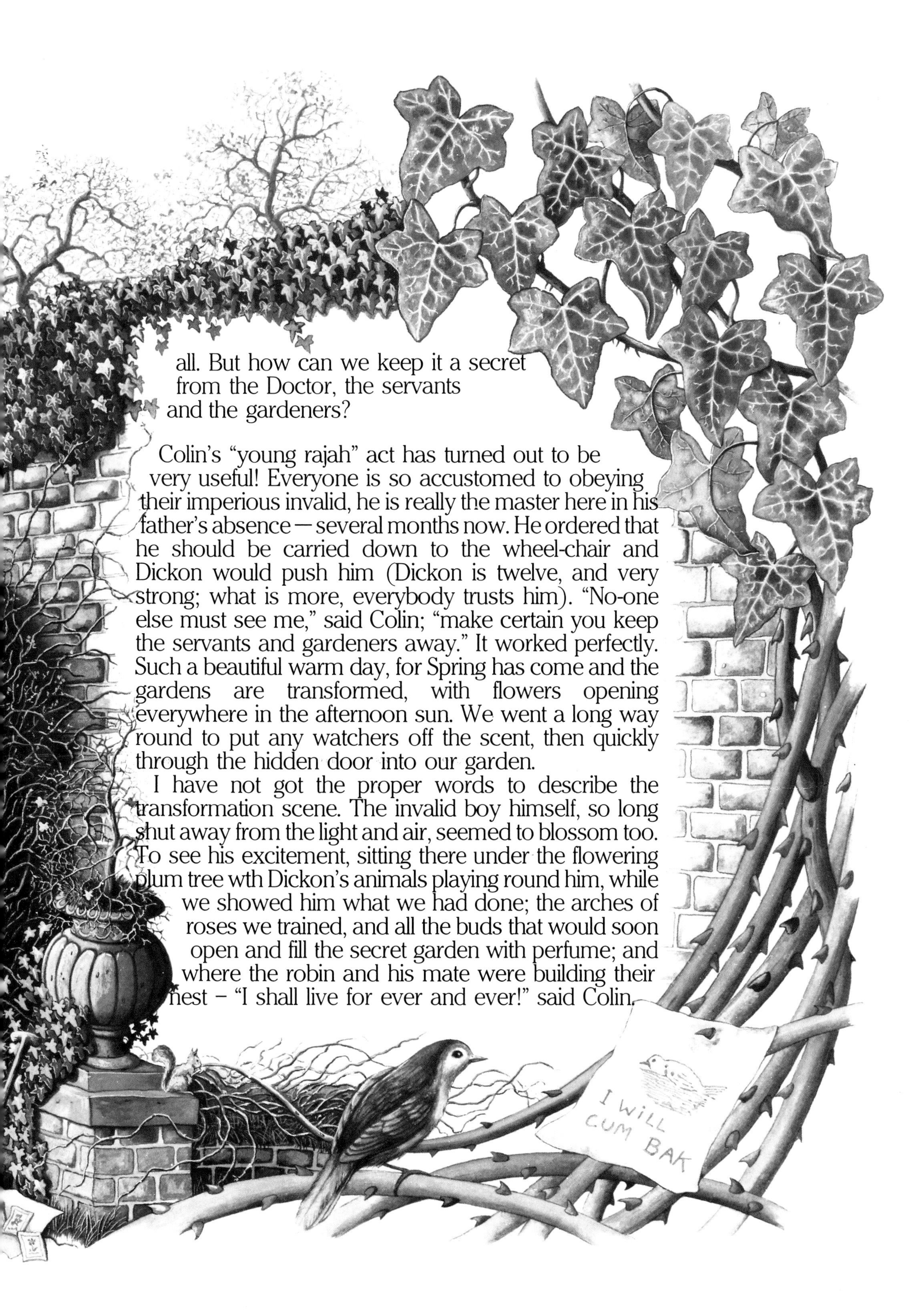

all. But how can we keep it a secret from the Doctor, the servants and the gardeners?

Colin's "young rajah" act has turned out to be very useful! Everyone is so accustomed to obeying their imperious invalid, he is really the master here in his father's absence — several months now. He ordered that he should be carried down to the wheel-chair and Dickon would push him (Dickon is twelve, and very strong; what is more, everybody trusts him). "No-one else must see me," said Colin; "make certain you keep the servants and gardeners away." It worked perfectly. Such a beautiful warm day, for Spring has come and the gardens are transformed, with flowers opening everywhere in the afternoon sun. We went a long way round to put any watchers off the scent, then quickly through the hidden door into our garden.

I have not got the proper words to describe the transformation scene. The invalid boy himself, so long shut away from the light and air, seemed to blossom too. To see his excitement, sitting there under the flowering plum tree wth Dickon's animals playing round him, while we showed him what we had done; the arches of roses we trained, and all the buds that would soon open and fill the secret garden with perfume; and where the robin and his mate were building their nest – "I shall live for ever and ever!" said Colin.

Now it is high Summer, and the blossom on the fruit trees has given way to plums and little apples. We go to our secret garden every day; and it is still a secret. But it has become quite a game trying to hide Colin's progress from his official keepers, as he is determined to do. He is coming on so well: I know Winter must return some day and lock up the cold earth again, but Colin will never again be the shut-away hunchback that he was.

And the father who shut him away, and could not bear to look at him — what would he think if he saw him now?

THE SWORD IN THE STONE

"Merlyn's tower . . . was the highest room in the castle, directly below the look-out of the great tower, and from its window you could gaze across the open field — with its right of warren — across the park, and the chase, until your eye finally wandered out over the distant blue tree-tops of the Forest Sauvage."

I hope you appreciate how fortunate you are in having a very wise owl as your guide: none other than Archimedes himself, trusty companion of Merlyn the magician — his "familiar", in common parlance.

However, learned as I am, I shall try not to talk down to you: that would merely add another dimension in my already complicated existence. For, you see, Merlyn lives backwards in time. He is very old, but getting younger. He has already lived through *your* century; he remembers the excitement over the first flying machine and after that (before, really), the incredible steam-

engine; Isaac Newton in his orchard; the discovery of the New World — whatever that is. And he still smokes tobacco from that time: the Wart thought he was breathing fire!

Like the Wart (rhyming with Art, short for Arthur), I was only young when Merlyn found me; and was living with him in his cottage in the middle of the Forest Sauvage when the boy turned up. As, of course, the wizard knew he would; knew, moreover, this was his special pupil, the Once and Future King — But I anticipate.

Our cottage, with its well, was in a clearing. Half the downstairs was a stable for the white donkey. Above it, Merlyn's bedroom — also his study — was crammed from floor to ceiling with books, curios, gadgets, stuffed animals, and live ones: hedgehogs, badgers, caterpillars, a flourishing beehive — even an ants' nest under glass, and for me, his Familiar, he always kept a dead mouse or two under his wizard's hat.

I could see the Wart was amazed by this room; I was used to it, but it was like some fantastical museum to him. And when Merlyn did some of his ordinary magic — objects appearing on demand, or ordering the breakfast things to wash themselves up (wizards get terribly lazy) — the boy's eyes nearly popped right out!

I quite took to the lad — though naturally I kept my distance at first: a highly educated tawny owl, one, moreover, that can *talk*, must never forget his dignity.

Now it was time for young Wart's preparation to begin. We went back with him to the castle that day — taking all the animals, of course . . . Did I tell you he had been chasing a rogue falcon? It must have taken a lot of nerve: there's no knowing what wild beasts and savages inhabit that forest. Well, on our way, we spied it. Merlyn snared it craftily: not by magic, but with bait and noose ("You can't use magic in the Great Arts," he said); and after a joyful welcome it was returned to the Mews where the hawks are kept, as you may see in the picture.

The castle belonged to Sir Ector, the Wart's guardian, who had taken him in as a foundling baby. Nothing was known of his birth or lineage; and Sir Ector's son Kay would often tease his adopted younger brother. I never took to Kay: he was difficult and easily hurt, but cared little for the hurt he caused. His only dealings with animals were because riding and hawking were the Right Thing for a future knight. But the Wart loved them. He spent all his time in the castle mews and kennels, learning about falcons from old Hob the austringer, playing with the hounds and the Dog Boy who minded them, or helping with the horses. I often went mousing there, and even in winter it was warm and fragrant with straw and fur and the good smells of well-kept animals. The chink of harness and falcons' bells and the clump of heavy hooves (big steeds, you see, both to plough and to carry the weight of armour) were music to the boy — and far more interesting than Greek, Summulae Logicales or the wretched Astrolabe: what the pompous sergeant-at-arms who drilled them in jousting used to call "a First Rate Eddication."

The education Merlyn offered was of a very different

WAX

8.
7.
9.
6.
10.
5.
4.
3.
2.
11
12.
1.
SOUTH
Camp Of The Anthropophagi
Robin Wood's Camp
Madame Mim's Cottage
Archery
Jousting Field
Sir Ector's Castle

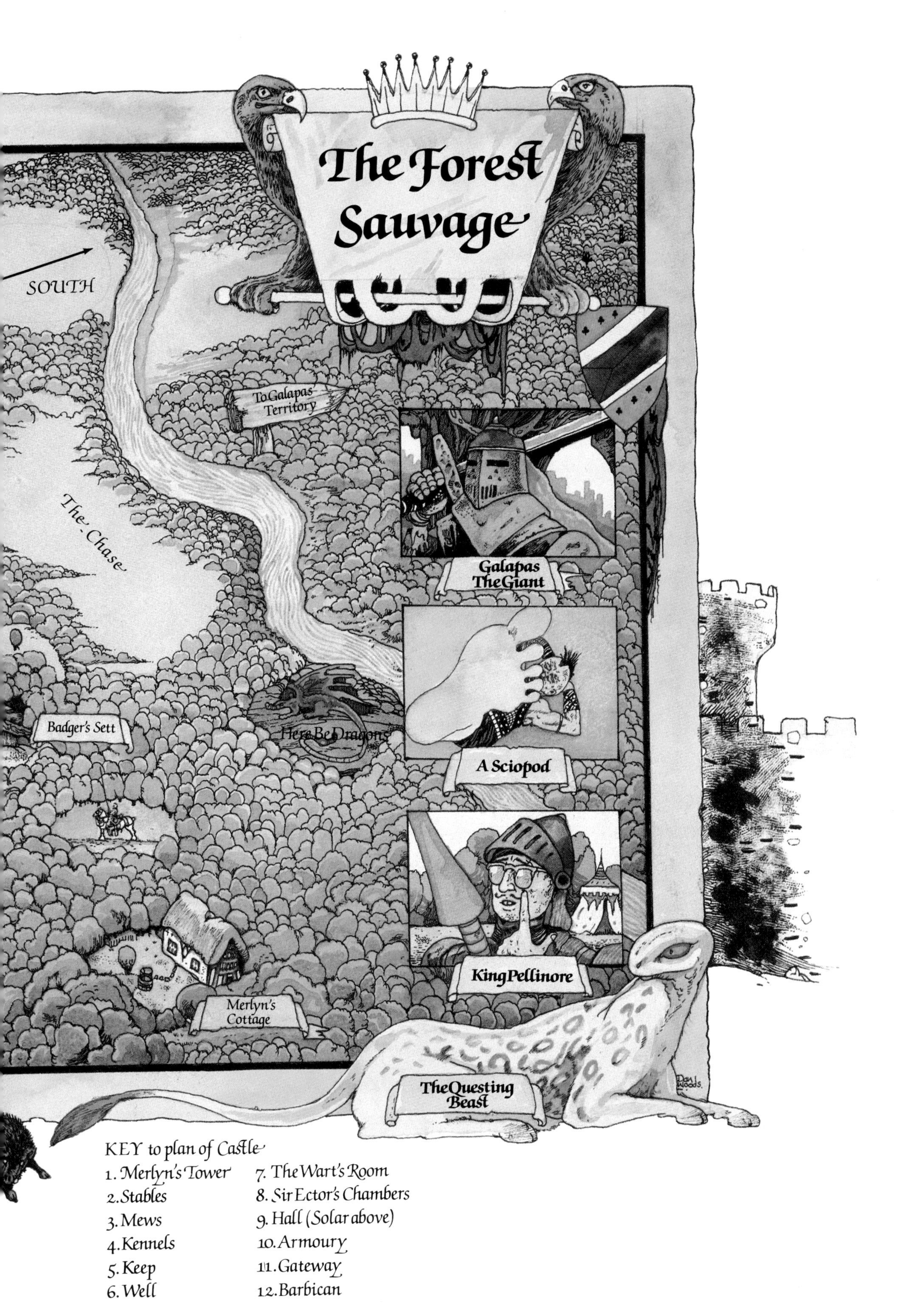
The Forest Sauvage
SOUTH
To Galapas Territory
The Chase
Badger's Sett
Here Be Dragons
Galapas The Giant
A Sciopod
King Pellinore
Merlyn's Cottage
The Questing Beast
KEY to plan of Castle
1. Merlyn's Tower
2. Stables
3. Mews
4. Kennels
5. Keep
6. Well
7. The Wart's Room
8. Sir Ector's Chambers
9. Hall (Solar above)
10. Armoury
11. Gateway
12. Barbican

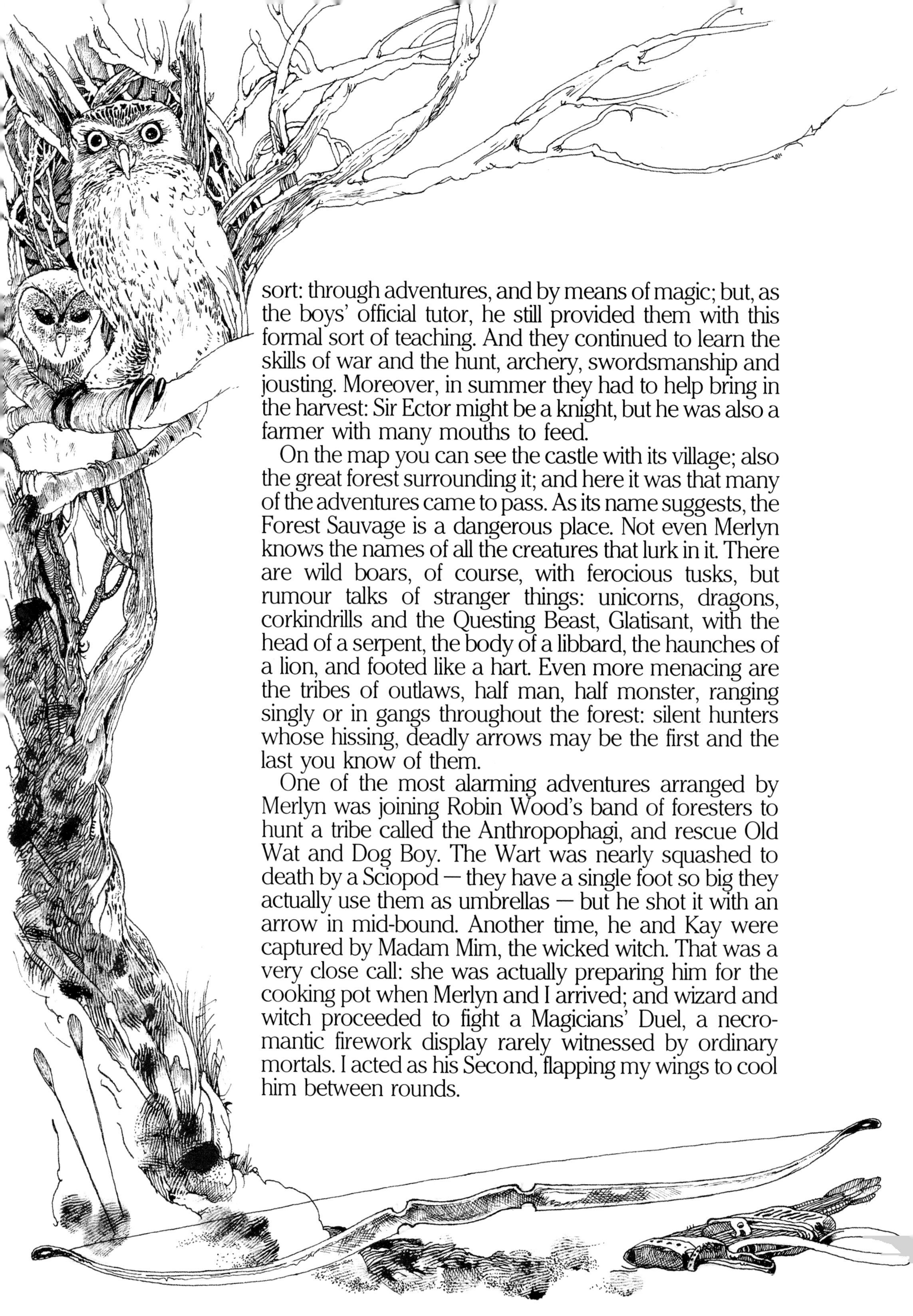

sort: through adventures, and by means of magic; but, as the boys' official tutor, he still provided them with this formal sort of teaching. And they continued to learn the skills of war and the hunt, archery, swordsmanship and jousting. Moreover, in summer they had to help bring in the harvest: Sir Ector might be a knight, but he was also a farmer with many mouths to feed.

On the map you can see the castle with its village; also the great forest surrounding it; and here it was that many of the adventures came to pass. As its name suggests, the Forest Sauvage is a dangerous place. Not even Merlyn knows the names of all the creatures that lurk in it. There are wild boars, of course, with ferocious tusks, but rumour talks of stranger things: unicorns, dragons, corkindrills and the Questing Beast, Glatisant, with the head of a serpent, the body of a libbard, the haunches of a lion, and footed like a hart. Even more menacing are the tribes of outlaws, half man, half monster, ranging singly or in gangs throughout the forest: silent hunters whose hissing, deadly arrows may be the first and the last you know of them.

One of the most alarming adventures arranged by Merlyn was joining Robin Wood's band of foresters to hunt a tribe called the Anthropophagi, and rescue Old Wat and Dog Boy. The Wart was nearly squashed to death by a Sciopod — they have a single foot so big they actually use them as umbrellas — but he shot it with an arrow in mid-bound. Another time, he and Kay were captured by Madam Mim, the wicked witch. That was a very close call: she was actually preparing him for the cooking pot when Merlyn and I arrived; and wizard and witch proceeded to fight a Magicians' Duel, a necromantic firework display rarely witnessed by ordinary mortals. I acted as his Second, flapping my wings to cool him between rounds.

For the Wart, many of these magical "lessons" started with being transformed into some animal — fish, owl, hawk, badger, snake — learning their mysterious skills, listening to their wisdom, playing their strange and dangerous game of survival. It gave him a new point of view — literally. Imagine having a snaky white swan break through your ceiling to peer down at you, or flying through the midnight sky observing the world below with an owl's night-vision, and learning how to land on a branch by rising and stalling.

There's one adventure whose location you won't find on the map: to visit Athena, goddess of wisdom — for that was a journey beyond space, into the vast deserts of time. The owl is Her emblem, Her pet. Young Wart was changed into one by swallowing a magic mouse (very much like a ripe peach with skin on), and I took him to Her shrine. Through Her vast wisdom he was able to hear the very rocks talking, telling of the birth of the world; and then the trees themselves whispering their ancient knowledge: oak, ash, beech, in their turn. That was, perhaps, the strangest of all the boy's journeyings; and I see nowadays, as I tell the tale to my own grandchildren (one is now at Court, I'd have you know, to keep the new king company and make messes in the soup), that Merlyn wanted the widest and deepest education for the Wart, to turn a rough-and-tumble lad, a mere fledgeling, into a wise ruler of men.

Meanwhile, he grew and learned the skills of men; he jousted and practised archery — he learned much from Robin about woodcraft — and joined in the winter boar-hunt. The castle was a wonderful place for boys to grow up in: a great warren of intricate defences, with its moat and drawbridge, its outer and inner ring of towers, its busy kitchens, a favourite place for dogs and boys, its mighty hall, with the comfortable solar above. Merlyn

and I lived in the highest tower of all, with a view across to the Welsh marches, and here the boys came for their formal lessons.

All too soon life changed. Kay was suddenly a knight, and the Wart his humble squire — a vassal, not a brother. As knight and squire they rode to the tourney in London, where all the best people were gathering: the old king had died, leaving no heir — only a sword in a stone: he who withdrew it would be King; and every man fancied his chance, and tried his hand in vain.

Kay was riding to the jousting field when he found he had left his sword behind. He sent his squire to get him another. Everywhere was closed: London had gone to the tourney. But the Wart knew he must not return empty-handed. In a churchyard he found a sword stuck into a stone: a sort of war memorial, he thought. No one will mind if I take it — so, here goes. . .

LITTLE WOMEN

"On one side was an old, brown house, looking rather bare and shabby, robbed of the vines that in summer covered its walls and the flowers which then surrounded it. On the other side was a stately stone mansion, plainly betokening every sort of comfort and luxury, from the big coach house and well kept grounds to the conservatory and glimpses of lovely things one caught between the rich curtains."

I spied on them so often I even knew their names. I could hear them playing in their jolly little gardens — they each had a quarter of the small plot, you see — and calling to one another. Meg was the eldest: a beauty, "outshining her simple homespun" like any proper heroine of Romance; and often accompanied by Amy, the youngest, a pocket edition with the same fair curls, and mightily pleased with herself: quite the little Madam. Beth, so fresh and quiet — smooth-haired, like a sweet madonna — was always busy caring for her family, including a hospital full of ailing dolls; and last but not least, there was Jo. She's my favourite: not a beauty really, but with the awkward grace of a long-leggedy chestnut colt — and always larking and getting into scrapes. She does have uncommonly nice hair, but not being one to fuss with her looks, she keeps it bundled up hugger-mugger in a sort of snood.

The suburbs where we live are quite open and countri-

fied, with the river nearby. My family name is Laurence (I'm Laurie to my friends as my real christian name, Theodore, is *too* dismal.) I live with my grandfather: just the two of us, apart from the servants of course. Our place is next door to the Marches; and though ours has rather a large garden and coach house and so on, it's quite close on that side. I could even see into their parlour — luckily for me they don't pull their curtains! — past the flowers in the window, to where their mother sat at teatime in the rosy glow of the firelight, with those four bright heads turned towards her. She looked so kind and comforting; and I wished she was mine. Mine's dead, you see — oh, ever so long ago now . . . But I did envy them just a little. I suppose it was rather sly to observe

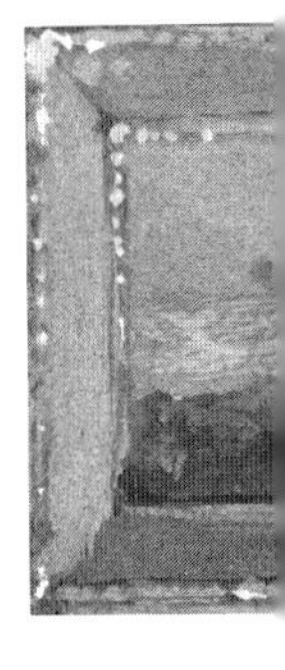

them so — but it didn't *feel* sneaky one bit! Through the long dark evenings when my grandfather was at his books, it was more like watching some enchanting play: that little parlour window all warm and brightly lit. The sort of play you know will have a happy ending.

It's the oddest thing how hard it is to cross barriers, break the ice and face the music (to mix a few "messy-paws", as Amy might say), and get to visit thy neighbour. Even though I'd met the older girls at the Andersons' Christmas party and got on pretty well, helping them out when Miss Meg gave her ankle a sad wrench, I'd never have got to know the Marches if Jo hadn't climbed through the hedge one afternoon and thrown a snowball at my window. I was languishing with a cold, dull as tombs and feeling abominably blue; and there she was. With her mother's permission she had came up to entertain the poor "prisoner", armed with a blancmange and an armful of kittens — much to the servants' surprise! Did me no end of good. She's a capital talker; and I heard all about the family, and how she was already a "business man", as she put it, helping support the little family, though she was but fifteen, like me — except, of course, that I'm her senior by several months. Their father is away at the war, you know: he volunteered as chaplain though he was over the age of conscription: he's something of a saint, is Mr March. Well, Jo's job, she told me, was being companion to a tetchy rich old Aunt — not to mention her fat poodle and an irrepressible parrot shrieking "Bless my boots! Aren't we fine! Get along you fright!" I laughed fit to bust — and quite forgot being ill and lonely.

I gathered she was mad on reading; so I showed her over the library, and the conservatory too, and loaded her up with flowers to take home. Even my grandfather, who returned suddenly, and who is not the easiest of guardians — avoiding company, and cornery when he

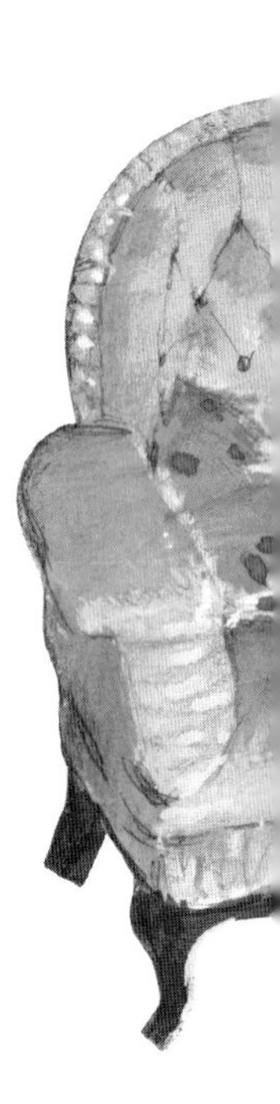

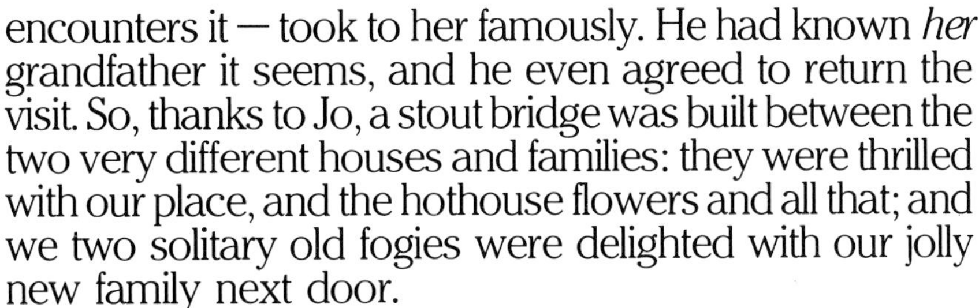

encounters it — took to her famously. He had known *her* grandfather it seems, and he even agreed to return the visit. So, thanks to Jo, a stout bridge was built between the two very different houses and families: they were thrilled with our place, and the hothouse flowers and all that; and we two solitary old fogies were delighted with our jolly new family next door.

Now that there were chums to do things with there was suddenly so much to do. There was skating on the river, or driving them out for rides in the carriage, or picnics in summer. One of the finest larks — not just 'cause I master-minded it! — was a river trip to Camp Laurence: some dozen of us in two boats rowed up to my prearranged camp-site, where there were tents and food and all (even a mown strip for croquet — it took some cunning preparation you see!); and we had a perfectly splendid day feasting, playing games, telling stories and rowing home in the sunset.

On wet days we held meetings of the Pickwick Club, or got up a play; Jo was a wizard at carpentering the scenery, as well as writing most of the melodrama, and all of them produced splendiferous costumes with the most amazing ingenuity, trimming cast-off hats and cloaks with bits and bobs, and even the curvy glittering diamonds of foil left over by the canning factory! One evening in winter we went to a real play, *The Seven Castles of the Silver Lake*, and enjoyed a charming spectacle: as many imps, elves, princes and princesses as the heart could wish. But, indirectly, that was the start of something that came near as a whisker to a tragedy. Amy, you see, wasn't allowed to go; and, in a fit of pique, she burnt Jo's Book — her own writings. Jo positively would not forgive her; and when we went skating next day, with Amy following along behind, she deliberately ignored her. The ice in the middle wasn't safe; I didn't see Amy and went on ahead... Well, Amy fell through the ice

and might have drowned: we only saved her in the nick of time. Jo was devastated and contrite — and once we had got the sad wet morsel home and warm by the fire, they hugged and made friends.

It's odd, but — amidst all the larks and the scrapes we got into — I see now how each of us seemed to come up against a sort of Test. For example Meg, being eldest, remembered most clearly the good times before their father lost all his money in the cause of an unfortunate friend; and felt most keenly the loss of luxury, the necessity for work; so when she was asked for a fortnight to the smart, rich Moffats, it quite went to her head. I was bidden to a party there, and I saw her all frizzed up and flirty; and I'm afraid I told her — well, that she was quite splendid but I simply didn't like fuss and feathers. But it must be fearfully hard, especially for a pretty girl — and when your friends are wealthy and idle, while you're poor and hardworking — not to enjoy being spoilt like a favourite doll . . . Of course I kept mum about the whole episode. Home and good sense gets one back to the real values.

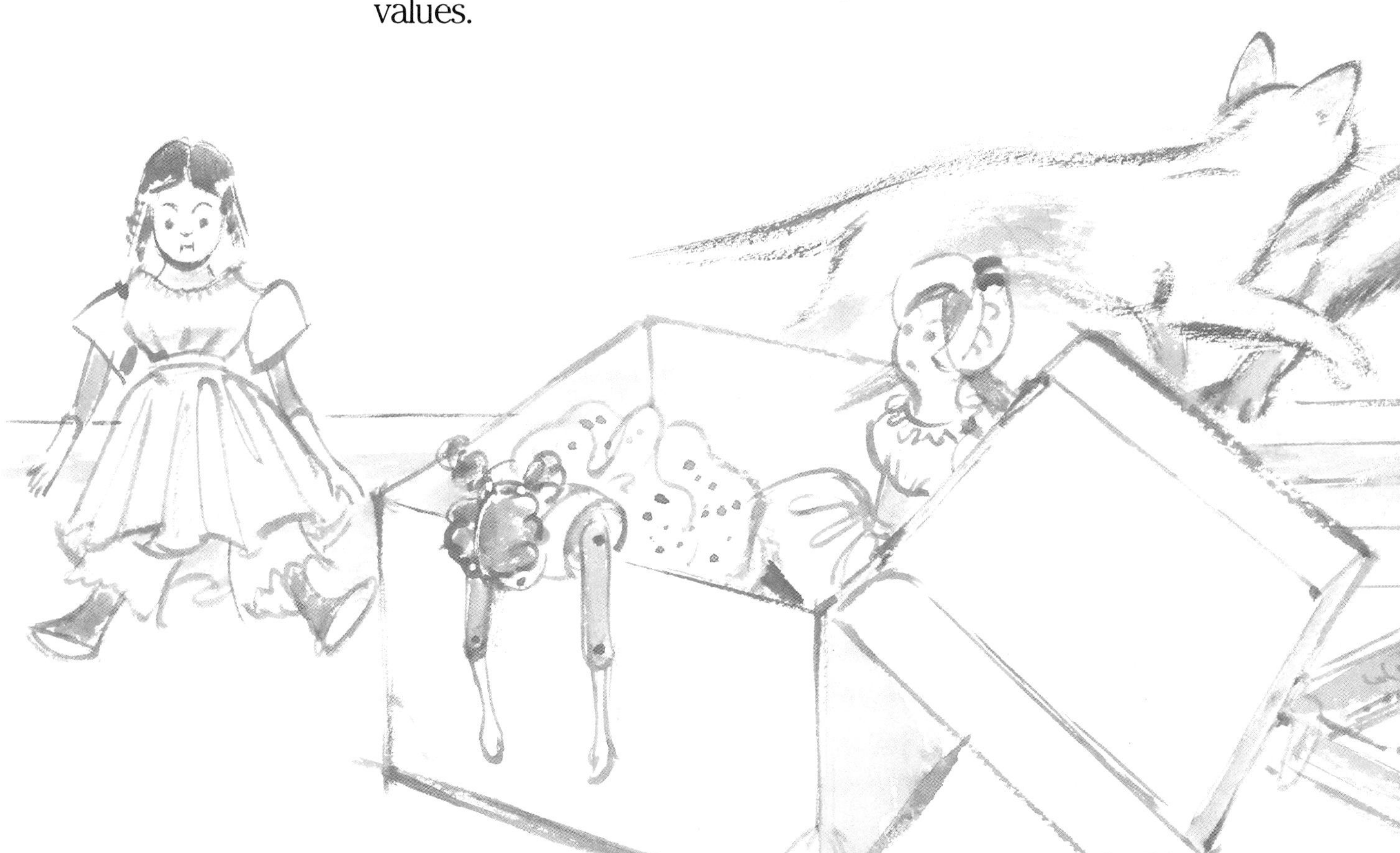

And I've no business anyway sounding so smug: I had ever so many ups and downs. My worst down started with a splendid prank (as I thought) and very nearly ended in my running away to sea! My tutor, Brooke — a capital fellow — had been somewhat smitten by the fair Meg; so I wrote her a lovering letter purporting to be from him. She answered it in good faith — then cottoned on; and that well and truly set the cat amongst the pigeons. I was abjectly sorry, and they forgave me after a regular talking-to; but my grandfather, who is really a dear old chap, heard about it and punished me: gave me a shaking as though I were a mere child, and sent me to my room. If I detest anything it's being lorded over: I had eaten my humble pie, and I was hanged if I was going to be lectured and pummelled; and I was quite determined to run away for ever — but Jo made the peace between us. She understands, as she had a dreadful temper herself; the girls say they like to get Jo into a fury: she's such an angel afterwards! But little Beth is really the only angel amongst us.

On a summer's afternoon they would sometimes take their portable tasks — household mending, or knitting for the soldiers — as bundles on their backs, out through the garden gate, across the meadow (an odd little procession) and up the hill to the clump of pine trees, with its view over the river and the town. One day up there we fell to talking of "castles-in-the-air". I dreamed of settling in Germany and becoming a famous musician; Amy, of being an artist in Rome. Meg wanted a house of her very own, luxury, clothes and servants, and — when pressed upon by the others — yes, even a husband and children, maybe. Jo's castle was all stablefuls of Arab steeds, staterooms piled with books, and a magic inkwell; and Beth's was simply "to stay at home with Mother and Father — and my little piano": a modest enough "cottage-in-the-air" — but even this was nearly taken from her by a cruel stroke of fate.

Jo's "magic inkwell", however, was about to materialise. After the burning of her magnum opus, she simply redoubled her efforts, writing hard in every spare moment. Not only did she pen the melodramas we staged, but she was the driving force behind the aforementioned Pickwick Club. Meetings of this august and exclusive society were held in the large attic room. Meg, as eldest, was naturally Mr Pickwick himself, and chairman; Jo was Snodgrass; and the main business was the reading of the minutes and newsletter, made up of verses, stories, reports of happenings and editorial comment on individual conduct.

But the smaller attic room was Jo's "garret"; and here she used to scribble away by the hour, spreading out her papers on the old tin trunk that was both her desk and her locker, to guard her manuscripts from the all-too-friendly rats. No one suspected what was afoot, until I bumped into her in town one day behaving in a singularly odd and secretive manner. I wormed it out of her; and

the great day came when the newspaper published a story called *The Rival Painters*. I must say, it was splendid to be in on the lark when she read it out to the family, then quietly admitted it was *Hers!* What unbottling of rapture that was!

Dear Jo may not be what Amy calls *"commy la fo"*, but she's a capital fellow; and I felt really proud of her when their father got home at last after his worrying illness, and 'specially praised his tomboy for her odd and touching sacrifice: having all that pretty hair cut off to sell for twenty-five dollars to send him to help pay for medical care... And how splendid it is to see the family complete at last; and the careful Beth putting out *two* pairs of slippers to warm by that cosy hearth, in the happiest home I know.

CHARLOTTE'S WEB

"The barn was very large. It was very old. It smelled of hay and it smelled of manure. It smelled of the perspiration of tired horses and the wonderful sweet breath of patient cows."

Why not "Some Rat"? That's what I want to know. Why didn't Charlotte ever write about *me* in her web? Why was it always that pig? Oh, Wilbur's all right, I guess, but he is only a pig, while I, Templeton, am quite a superior rat.

Not that I ever wanted to be famous. We rats don't care for fame, for being stared at and made to do tricks. We prefer to stay out of sight, eating, gnawing and watching, keeping our bellies full and our backs warm. I don't expect the visitors to Zuckerman's barn to think of me. Let them gossip and giggle about Wilbur and the spider. I don't want their attention. But I do think I deserve a little gratitude.

Wilbur makes such a fuss about how Charlotte saved his life, but he forgets that I saved Charlotte. When that awful boy, Avery, came towards Charlotte with a big stick, what stopped him and made him run away? It was the smell of the rotten goose egg, when he tripped and smashed it. And who was it who kept the goose egg when nobody else wanted it? Who was it who hid it underneath Wilbur's trough, knowing it would come in handy some day? Only me. Yet what thanks did I get?

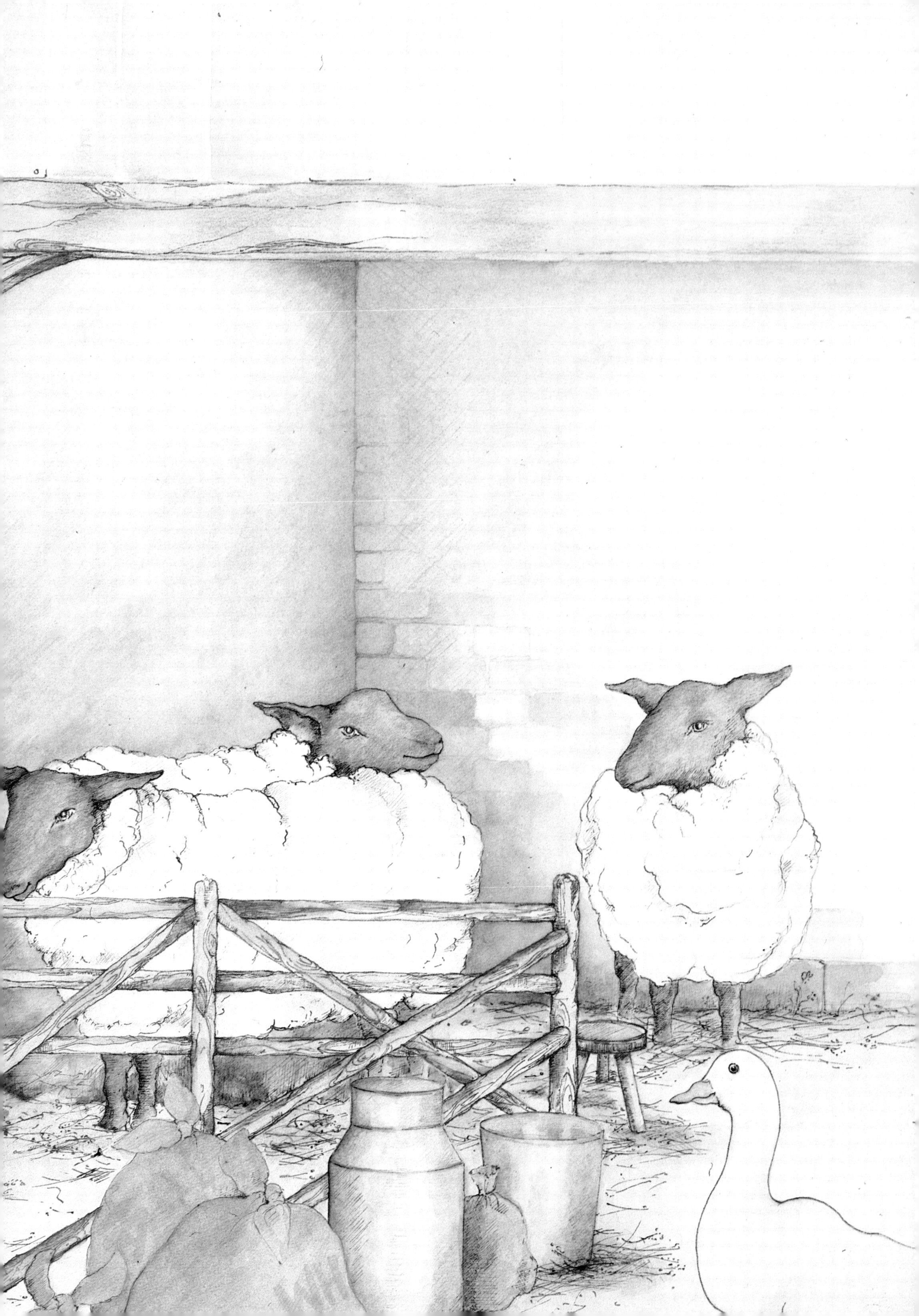

What thanks does a rat ever get?

Yes, this is the doorway where Charlotte hung her web. I think you can still see some pieces of it, although why anyone cares beats me. This old barn is full of cobwebs, and none of them is good for anything but catching flies. My own treasures are a lot more useful.

I'll show you around if you like. I'm the one to ask if you have any questions. I know more about this barn than the man who built it. I know this place upstairs and down, inside and out, and even underground, through my tunnels. What I can't tell you about the barn isn't worth knowing.

To start with the most interesting part, here, in the

fenced yard just outside the barn, is my trough.

That's Wilbur's trough, you say? Oh, no. Not now. Wilbur and I have a deal: I go first at meal-times, and he eats *my* left-overs. I say that makes it mine.

Before the change in ownership, I used to have my lair beneath the trough, and spent a lot of time there. Wilbur was always a sloppy eater, so some of the best bits fell down to me. I lined my nest cosily with bits of this and that — potato peelings, bird feathers, wool, candy wrappers — and it always smelled deliciously of rotting food. But getting all I want to eat has made me quite a bit bigger, and these days I find my old lair a tight fit. I suppose I could enlarge it, but that would mean hard work, and I prefer to save my strength for meal-times.

My new nest is up in the loft, behind one of the grain bins. Though I say it myself, I've never seen a more perfect rat's nest. Lying there snug at night I can hear the cows chewing their cuds and the horses shifting and breathing heavily in their stalls. The only place warmer in winter might be the manure pile, down in the cellar where Wilbur and the sheep live. But the loft is much cooler in summer, because then the big doors are left open and there's always a breeze.

If you'll promise not to touch anything, I'll let you peep into my nest. It's not just a hobby, this collection of mine, you know — it's a way of life. Some may sneer, but you never know when a piece of string, an old goose egg, a greasy cheese wrapper or a mouldy piece of bread might come in handy, or even save somebody's life. I'm sure you'll agree my nest is far more interesting than any spider's web!

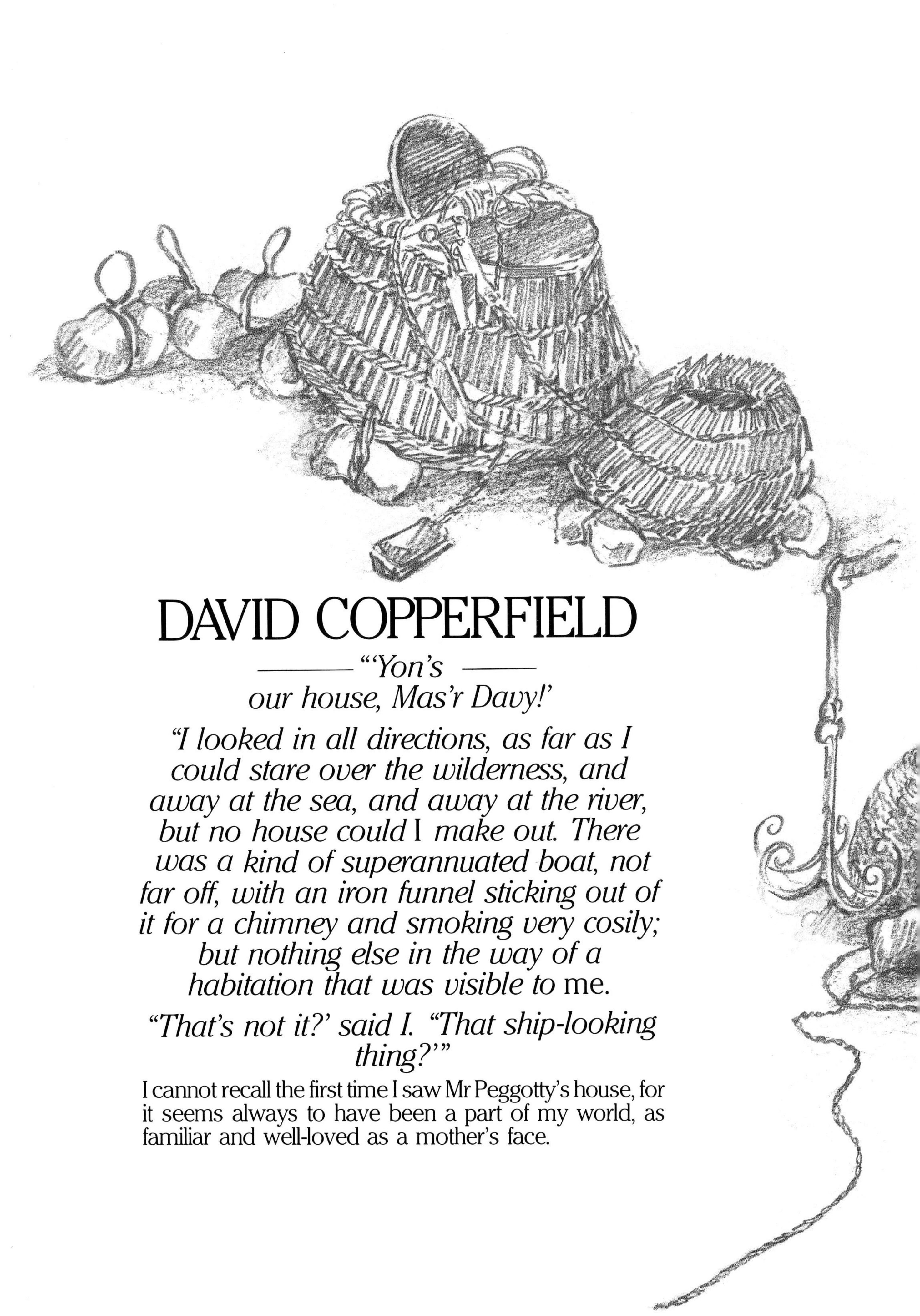

DAVID COPPERFIELD

"'Yon's our house, Mas'r Davy!'

"I looked in all directions, as far as I could stare over the wilderness, and away at the sea, and away at the river, but no house could I *make out. There was a kind of superannuated boat, not far off, with an iron funnel sticking out of it for a chimney and smoking very cosily; but nothing else in the way of a habitation that was visible to* me.

"That's not it?' said I. "That ship-looking thing?'"

I cannot recall the first time I saw Mr Peggotty's house, for it seems always to have been a part of my world, as familiar and well-loved as a mother's face.

I knew the people who lived in the boat-house only by sight. There was a neat, thin, prim little body in a white apron called Mrs Gummidge; a sheepish, curly-haired, gangling boy named Ham; and a pretty little girl, about two years younger than I was, known as little Em'ly. Looking after them all was the hearty, hairy, good-natured fisherman, Daniel Peggotty. He had a sister, Clara, who worked as a nurse for a family in Suffolk, and I remember the time she turned up with a little boy in tow; "Mas'r Davy", they called him, a young gentleman.

My chance to befriend Emily came a few years later, when we were both at school. Some of the other girls thought Emily gave herself airs, but to me it was only right. Anyone so fortunate to live where she did must be as wonderful as a princess.

One day little Em'ly invited me home for tea. If I live to be one hundred I shall never forget that glorious day — glorious in my mind only, I should say, for it was dreary, chilly November, and as we left school the air was cold

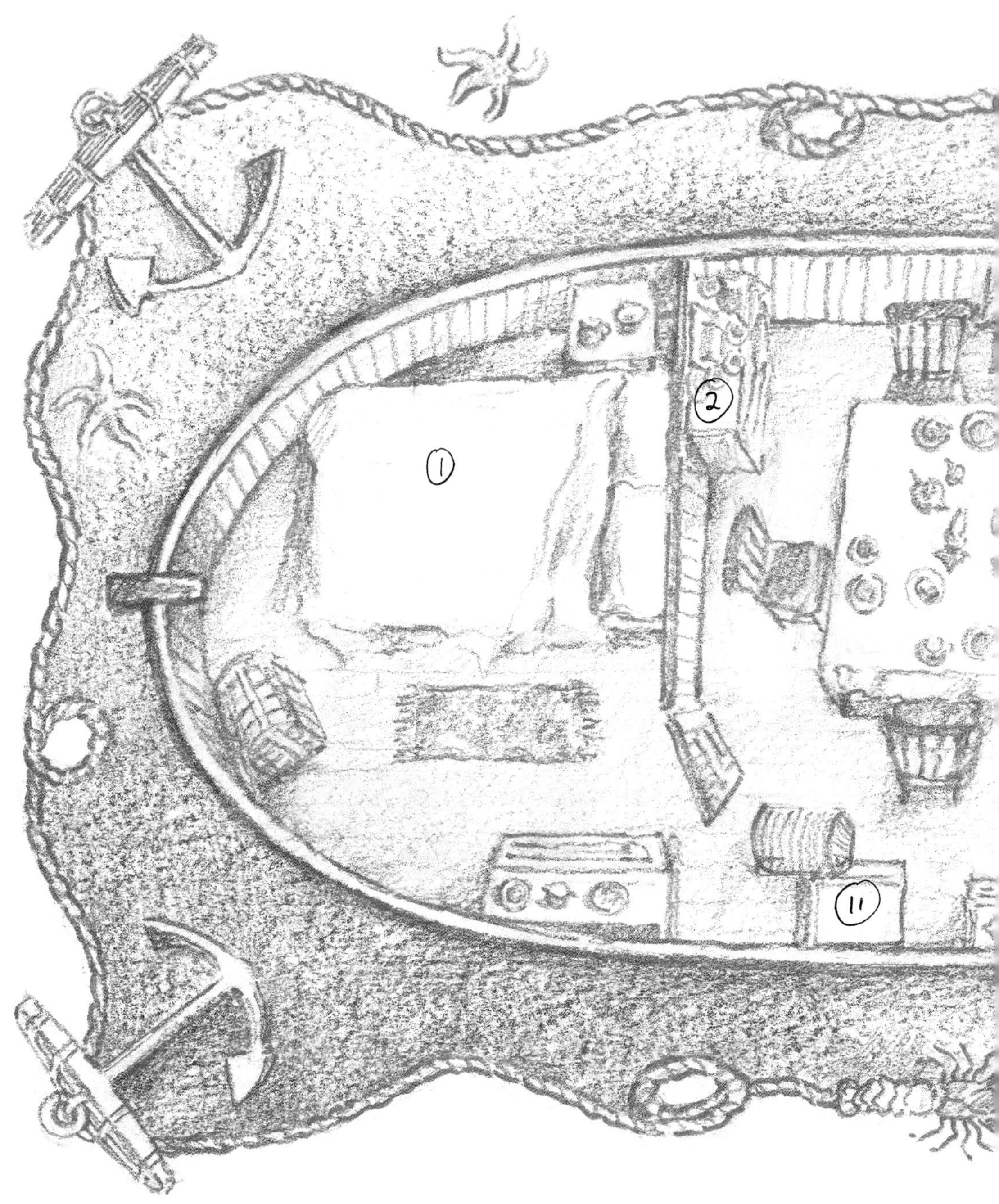

1. MRS. GUMMIDGE & LITTLE EM'LY'S BED
2. TEA TRAY ARRANGEMENT
3. LITTLE EM'LY'S LOCKER SEAT
4. FIREPLACE
5. GUEST BEDROOM
6. WINDOW

and damp and quickly darkening. We hurried over the hard-packed sand, drawn by the brave, flickering gleam of a candle in the dusk.

"There," said Em'ly at the sight of it, "That means Uncle Dan is home, for he always sets a candle in the window to let me know he is waiting".

Soon the solid bulk of the old boat loomed before us. My heart beat faster as Emily opened the door: at last I would see my dream in waking life.

I wanted to take it all in at one, greedy glance. I saw a perfect, cosy interior, all ship-shape as the sailors say.

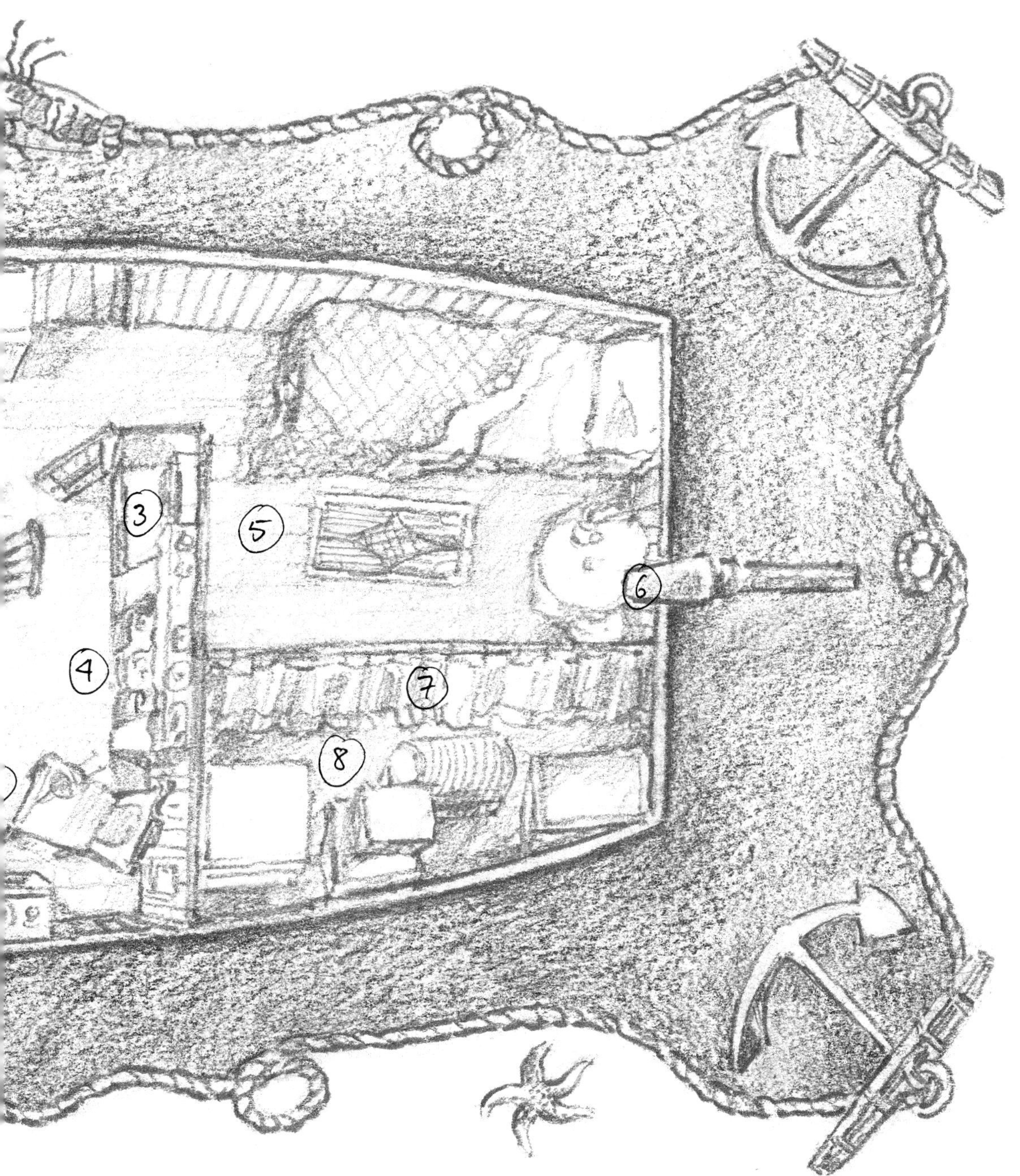

Everything was neatly in place and spotlessly clean. My first eager look around took in the wooden walls and the heavier beams of the ceiling, curving around us like ribs, and I thought of Jonah inside the whale. The furniture was plain and old-fashioned: a wooden table and chairs, a dresser, a Dutch clock. A cheerful fire was burning in the grate, and there were some brightly coloured pictures of Biblical subjects on the walls, but what particularly caught my attention was a depiction of a ship called the *Sarah Jane* which hung above the mantelshelf. This was no ordinary painting, for it had a real wooden stern stuck

(7) CURTAIN
(8) STORE ROOM
(9) MRS. GUMMIDGE'S KNITTING CHAIR
(10) WELSH DRESSER
(11) STORAGE FOR DAN & HAM'S HAMMOCKS

Gummidge, and a hearty, delicious meal it was, too: piles of boiled dabs served with melted butter, boiled potatoes, carrots, thick slices of bread and steaming mugs of sweet, milky tea. When we couldn't eat another bit we left the table to move closer to the fire.

Mr Peggotty settled in one chair with his pipe, and Mrs Gummidge in another with her knitting, while Ham was on the floor with some chore — mending a lobster pot, I

believe. There were a number of lockers and boxes about the place which served for seats as well as for storage, and the smallest of the lockers fitted snugly into the chimney corner. This was obviously little Em'ly's customary seat, and I was touched by her kindness in sharing it with me.

Gazing into the dancing flames, feeling the warmth while I listened to the rising wind and pounding sea outside, I truly knew my good fortune. I was snug and safe — this ship could weather any storm. With Mr Peggotty to steer her, we would never be in danger. For once in my life I knew what it was to be content, and to feel at home.

"You're happy here, aren't you?" said little Em'ly, close to my ear.

I nodded, my heart too full for words.

"Stay with us," said Em'ly. "Stay and be my sister. We'll help each other, and look after each other. Think how happy we could be! Shall I ask my uncle?"

But I shook my head. I was older than Emily and, if not wiser, at least more learned in the ways of the world. Children could not choose where they would live, and I knew that even if Dan Peggotty was kind enough to offer to take me, my relatives would not let me go. I had a home, even if I did not like it. Instead of explaining my thoughts, though, I only said, "But where could I stay? This house is too small for anyone else."

"Why, you silly!" cried Emily. "You haven't seen! You shall have the room where Davy stayed, for he is not here now and does not need it." She grasped my hand and jumped up, pulling me with her.

She opened a little door and revealed, tucked into the stern of the boat, a bedroom that anyone might envy. It

was precisely big enough for one, particularly if that one were small, as I was. Tucked against the wall, beneath a colourful patchwork spread, was a snug little bed. Above it was a mirror framed with oyster shells, and a small window, where once the boat's rudder must have passed through. The room was sparsely but brightly decorated with white-washed walls, pretty curtains, a rug, and a table bearing a blue mug full of dried seaweed. No palace in my imagination could have glowed more brightly or been more comfortable.

If only it could have been mine! How different my life might have been if I had grown up safe and secure in that odd, land-bound boat.

But the past is over and cannot be altered. Little Em'ly and my young self both have vanished. We are older, wiser, sadder women now, and all is changed.

But one thing I think is still the same, and that is Mr Peggotty's old boat-house. The people who once lived there have scattered now, but I am certain the house still stands on Yarmouth sands all by itself, a bulwark against the night, the weather, and time. I have only to close my eyes to see it again, to see the candle flickering bravely in the window as darkness gathers. And I know that if I could open the door I would find the room within unchanged, like the features of a well-loved face, ready to welcome me in. There will always be a place for me there, beside little Em'ly, on the locker in the chimney corner, safe from the storm.

JOHNNY TREMAIN

"There was only one window in the attic. Johnny always stood before it as he dressed. He like this view down the length of Hancock's Wharf. Counting-houses, shops, stores, sail lofts, and one great ship after another, home again after their voyaging, content as cows waiting to be milked. He watched the gulls, so fierce and beautiful, fighting and screaming among the ships. Beyond the. wharf was the sea and the rocky islands where gulls nested.

Here on Hancock's Wharf the smells are just the same after eighteen years: tar and salt water, a whiff of rubbish, fish drying in the sun, woodsmoke and smouldering charcoal. The sounds are the same, too: the crying and scolding of gulls wheeling overhead, waves slapping against the ships at anchor, sailors and traders shouting, wandering chickens clucking underfoot.

The house on Fish Street, at the head of the wharf, still stands. There is the attic window where I lingered to gaze at seagulls flying in the blue air, free as I thought I would never be, and at the tangled forest of masts and sails, dreaming my quiet dreams until it was "Look sharp,

Dusty!" from Johnny Tremain, and I had to scamper to my tasks.

I could almost believe, standing here, that no time has passed.

But I am no longer a boy, no longer apprenticed to Mr Lapham the silversmith, and everything has changed. The long war for independence is over. I am a free man, a merchant sailor with money to spend, and I've promised my wife a special gift from Boston: a silver christening cup for our new daughter. I had thought to go to Paul Revere, the finest craftsman in silver, but curiosity

brought me back here instead, to this small house where I once lived and worked.

Old Mr Lapham is dead now, but I learned in town that his widowed daughter-in-law – who used to call me a lazy good-for-nothing – kept the business in the family by marrying his partner, Mr Percival Tweedie.

Mrs Tweedie answers the door when I knock: she isn't as enormous as I remember, but still very stout, and her age shows in her white hair and the stooping way she stands. She doesn't know me, but sees my fine clothes and hears the way I jingle coins in my pocket as I declare I have business with the silversmith, and she is all

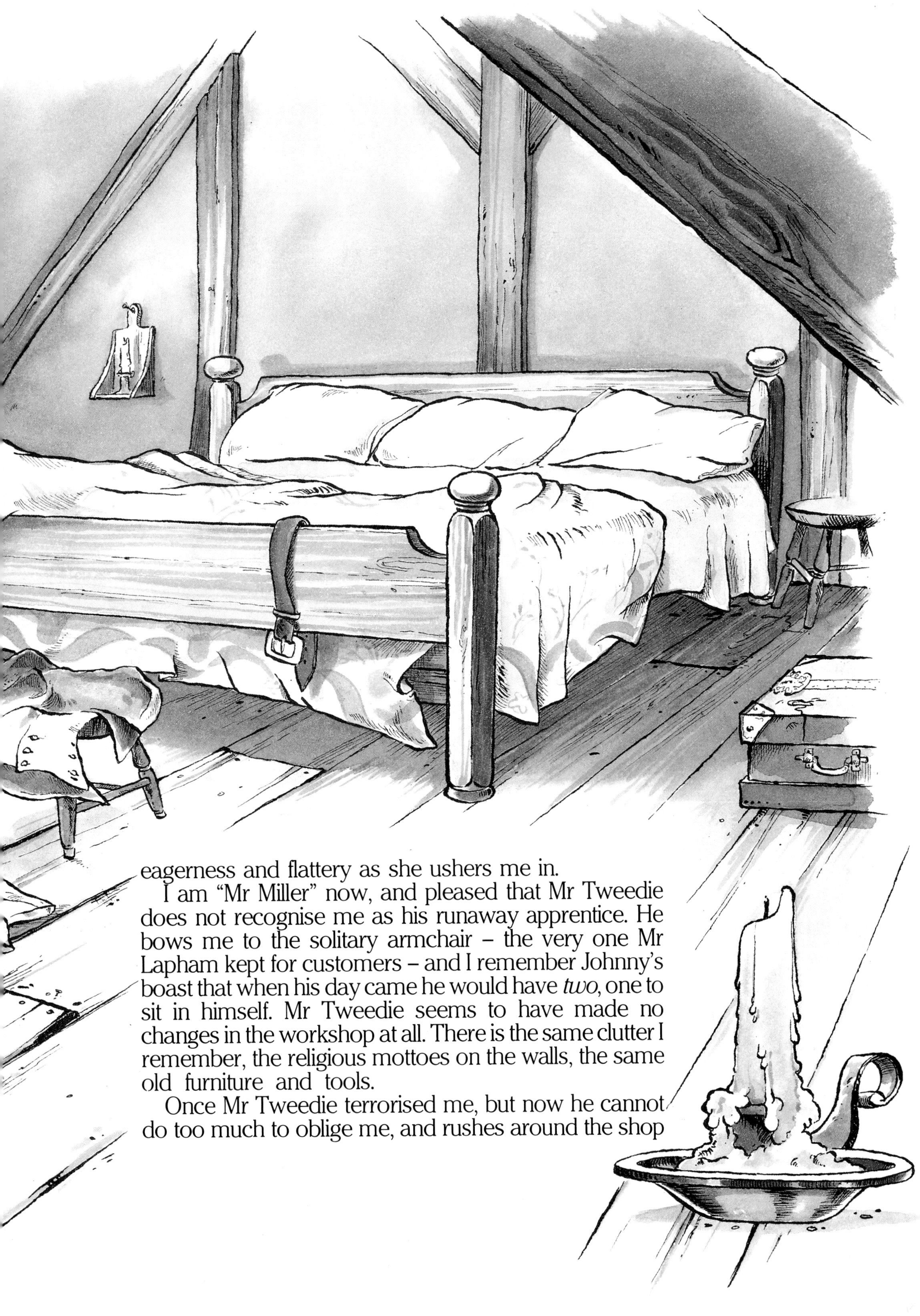

eagerness and flattery as she ushers me in.

I am "Mr Miller" now, and pleased that Mr Tweedie does not recognise me as his runaway apprentice. He bows me to the solitary armchair – the very one Mr Lapham kept for customers – and I remember Johnny's boast that when his day came he would have *two*, one to sit in himself. Mr Tweedie seems to have made no changes in the workshop at all. There is the same clutter I remember, the religious mottoes on the walls, the same old furniture and tools.

Once Mr Tweedie terrorised me, but now he cannot do too much to oblige me, and rushes around the shop

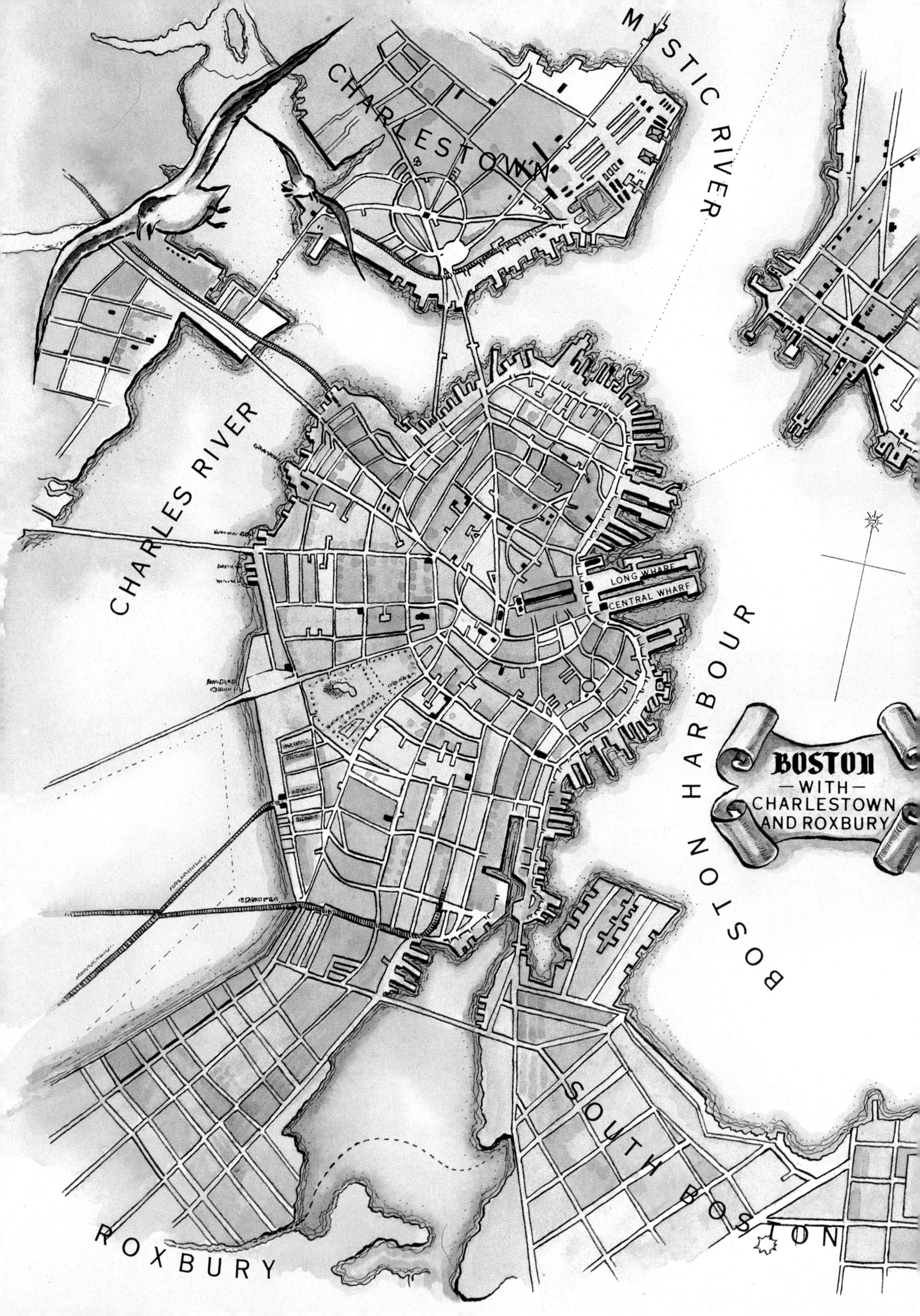
BOSTON
WITH
CHARLESTOWN
AND ROXBURY
CHARLESTOWN
MYSTIC RIVER
CHARLES RIVER
LONG WHARF
CENTRAL WHARF
BOSTON HARBOUR
SOUTH BOSTON
ROXBURY

gathering up odd bits of silverware, mugs, spoons, a coffee-pot. As I examine each one a combination of the shop's atmosphere (smells of charcoal, dust and hot silver) and the smooth, cool metal gleaming beneath my fingertips, sends my mind back to the days when I worked here.

I think about the kitchen, where Mrs Lapham fed us hearty, sustaining meals around the big table, and I wonder if the attic above is still the same, cramped, stuffy room where I shared a sagging bed with the other two apprentices, Dove and Johnny.

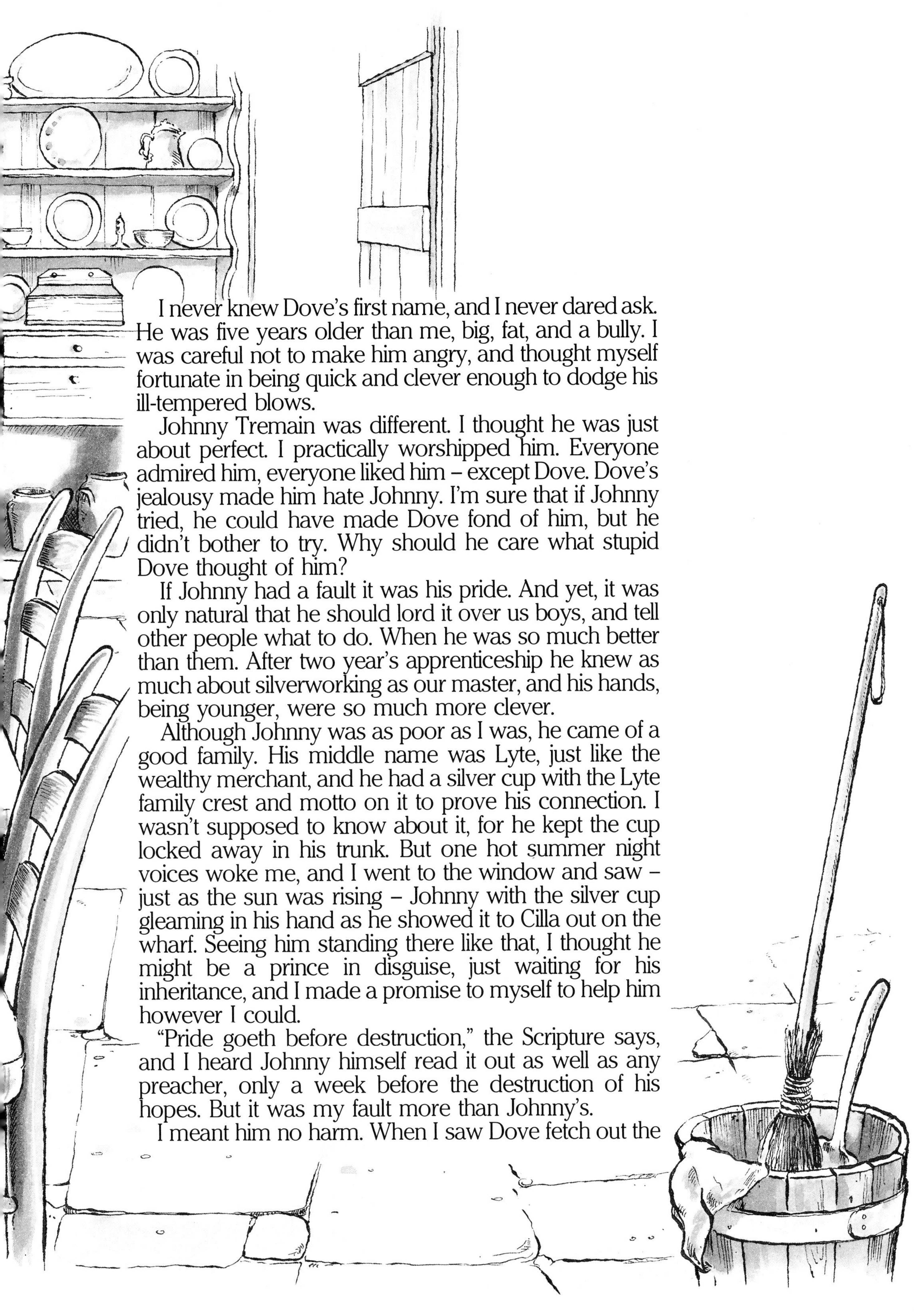

I never knew Dove's first name, and I never dared ask. He was five years older than me, big, fat, and a bully. I was careful not to make him angry, and thought myself fortunate in being quick and clever enough to dodge his ill-tempered blows.

Johnny Tremain was different. I thought he was just about perfect. I practically worshipped him. Everyone admired him, everyone liked him – except Dove. Dove's jealousy made him hate Johnny. I'm sure that if Johnny tried, he could have made Dove fond of him, but he didn't bother to try. Why should he care what stupid Dove thought of him?

If Johnny had a fault it was his pride. And yet, it was only natural that he should lord it over us boys, and tell other people what to do. When he was so much better than them. After two year's apprenticeship he knew as much about silverworking as our master, and his hands, being younger, were so much more clever.

Although Johnny was as poor as I was, he came of a good family. His middle name was Lyte, just like the wealthy merchant, and he had a silver cup with the Lyte family crest and motto on it to prove his connection. I wasn't supposed to know about it, for he kept the cup locked away in his trunk. But one hot summer night voices woke me, and I went to the window and saw – just as the sun was rising – Johnny with the silver cup gleaming in his hand as he showed it to Cilla out on the wharf. Seeing him standing there like that, I thought he might be a prince in disguise, just waiting for his inheritance, and I made a promise to myself to help him however I could.

"Pride goeth before destruction," the Scripture says, and I heard Johnny himself read it out as well as any preacher, only a week before the destruction of his hopes. But it was my fault more than Johnny's.

I meant him no harm. When I saw Dove fetch out the

cracked crucible, I giggled and said nothing. I knew that the heat of the furnace might split the crucible when Johnny set it down, and that the melted silver inside would spill out. I thought that Johnny would be scolded for his carelessness, just as Dove and I so often were. But I never imagined that Johnny would be hurt. How could I know that he would slip, and reach out his hand, towards the molten silver, and . . . How could I know that he would burn his hand so badly as to be useless as a silversmith? Had I guessed such a thing was possible, I would never have let it happen.

If I had spoken out and stopped the disaster, this would be Johnny's business now, not Mr Tweedie's, and instead of sitting here as a customer, I would be at the work-bench, the crimping iron in my hand, making something beautiful. I would be a silversmith, too – Johnny's trusted partner.

After Johnny left, nothing went right in this house again. Tweedie was a hard master, and Dove was a bully, and Mrs Lapham shouted, and my conscience nagged, and I missed Johnny. When I heard one day of a ship that needed a cabin boy, I took my chance and left, and never looked back, until now.

Suddenly I can't bear it. I push aside Tweedie's inferior silverware and leave the too-familiar shop, scarcely aware of his protests and worried questions. My mind is not on the present, but on the past, on Johnny and the little boy I once was. All I can think is how different everything might have been, if not for that broken sugar-bowl, that cracked crucible, and my silence.

ROBINSON CRUSOE

"There was a hill not above a mile from me, which rose up very steep and high, and which seemed to over-top some other hills, which lay as in a ridge from it northwards; . . . armed and with great difficulty I got to the top (and) saw to my affliction that I was in an island environed everyway with the sea, no land to be seen, except some rocks which lay about three leagues to the west."

You asked me, Mr Defoe, how must it feel to find yourself alone, like the last man left alive in the world. My circumstances were somewhat different from the plight of the man who saved my life, whom you name "Crusoe", but I can tell you this: the person that finds himself abandoned on a desert island is struck at once, in the first flush of his amazement at being alive, by the sheer magnificence around him; next, by the dreadful awe of being so alone – and only later, as night falls, that he may *not* be alone.

Imagine if you can his first hours on that lonely isle – and I have all too clear a knowledge of such despair: of that dawning realisation, as I sat on the shore with my head in my hands, that willy-nilly this savage place was to be my prison; that here I must somehow live and probably die – maybe violently and soon. I remember looking around me and being stricken as much by its extraordinary beauty as by its alien wildness: the blue

and sparkling sea turning to purest aquamarine in the shallows, the soft sand beneath me, the richly wooded shore, giving way to lofty pastures and sublime peaks – all seemed full of promise, of provisions. Yet what fierce beasts might dwell there? What savages might those woods conceal? So the more I marvelled at this desert paradise, my lush cage, the more I feared it might not be deserted . . . So *he* felt, dear sir; and so he described his feelings to me on that island. Having seen the home he created, I believe that what saved the sanity of Robinson Crusoe was simply being busy: working to survive. And it was these very fears that spurred him on.

You will have heard how his ship was wrecked, he the sole survivor cast up on the shore; how when night came he grew fearful and climbed a tree for safety from wild beasts, and how on awakening he saw to his joy that the ship had drifted onto the rocks within a mile of the shore. There followed many days of hard labour salvaging all he could from her by means of the rafts he built out of her masts and timbers, and floated ashore. What must have been his urgency to save such a sudden wealth of goods! Food, clothing, writing materials, tools and nails, arms and ammunition, good sailcloth and bedding, a hammock were all retrieved, and as much rope, chain, cable, twine and wood as he could amass once he had

the perishable items safely ashore – for he never could know how soon the wreck might be lost to him. Indeed, one brief heavy storm in the night and he woke to a sunlit, calm, but empty seascape.

His precious hard-won stores were now all he had or could hope for; and an unexpected bonus was the live companionship of the ship's dog, who swam ashore, and two cats, miraculously unharmed, that he carefully transported by raft to dry land – which they very quickly investigated; and soon made themselves at home. He followed suit, determined now to explore his new land, find a good place to live and build a dwelling more proof against rain and intruders than his makeshift tent. He told me, moreover, that exhausted as he was, the urge to busy himself from moment to moment was great, producing a welcome numbness to his circumstances; and he had to force himself to stop and take stock of his future needs. These he listed as follows: good water for the sake of his health, shelter from the hot sun, security from ravenous creatures, man or beast, and an open view of the sea – however faint his hopes of a ship to deliver him.

He found a place to suit these requirements: a grassy plain backed by a cliff, being the northwest side of a hill. Here he drew a wide half-circle for the line of his stockade, and started on the lengthy task of cutting big

stakes in the woods, transporting them and setting them in, only six inches apart, to make a high wall, weaving ships' cable between; during which time he kept his provisions covered and slept in his newly-pitched tent, with his dog and his cats, and a musket close at hand.

I wondered greatly at all his works as he showed me over the remarkable "castle" (as he called it) that had grown from these labours; and at the energy, determination and foresight that must be called upon even to set about such a task, let alone complete it. I said as much, and added: "It amazes me you did not despair." To which he replied: "I believe, sir, it became an end in itself; a pride, an obsession at times, in working out each project to the smallest detail, following it perfectly, with refinements along the way, and setting all down in my journal. At first a mere drug, these 'works of my hands' (as the Good Book terms it) became a Cause. Self-help was my salvation, and the nice fit of a bolt, or morticing of a joint, amounted to an act of creation."

I saw more "works of his hands" in the warren of caves he ingeniously hollowed out of the cliff: the cooking pots, storage jars and dishes he had formed from clay and baked in a slow fire under a clay cover; the baskets he had woven from reeds and withies – all filled with his

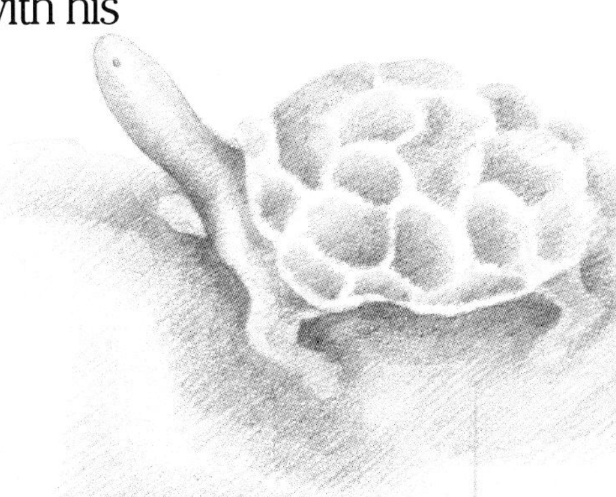

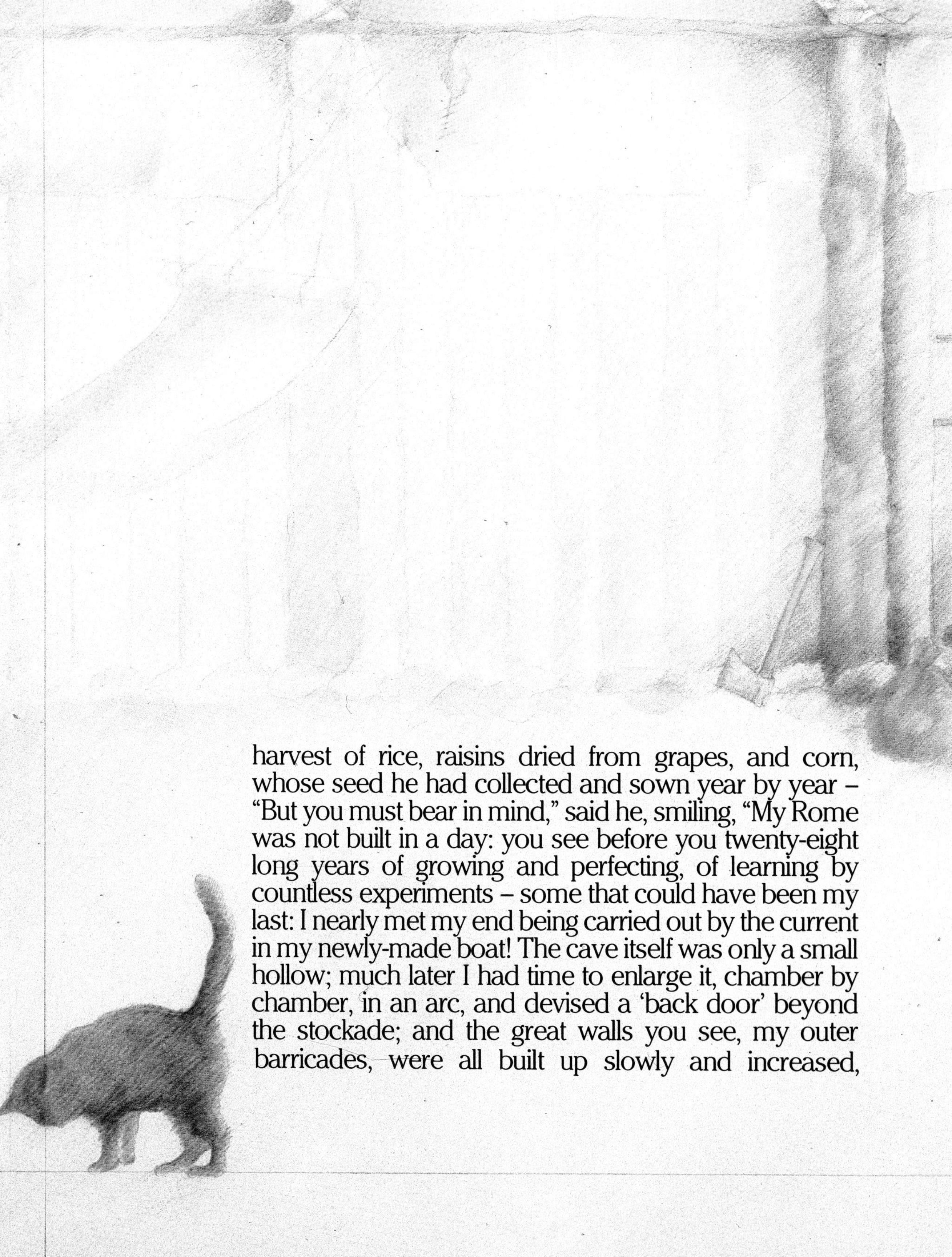

harvest of rice, raisins dried from grapes, and corn, whose seed he had collected and sown year by year – "But you must bear in mind," said he, smiling, "My Rome was not built in a day: you see before you twenty-eight long years of growing and perfecting, of learning by countless experiments – some that could have been my last: I nearly met my end being carried out by the current in my newly-made boat! The cave itself was only a small hollow; much later I had time to enlarge it, chamber by chamber, in an arc, and devised a 'back door' beyond the stockade; and the great walls you see, my outer barricades, were all built up slowly and increased,

particularly by the Growing-posts." These were stakes he had sunken which took root and now made a thicket of trees that quite hid his "castle" from all comers: not until the final stockade was reached could anyone see the holes cut in the impenetrable wall, a musket barrel in each. There was no door: only a retractable ladder.

Within this hidden fortress I found great domesticity and, indeed, comfort. The inner wall contained the dwelling of his native man "Friday", that excellent helpmeet and warrior (as we had witnessed in our own rescue), whom Crusoe had earlier saved from cannibal captors – scaring them with the lightning and thunder of his musket. The innermost section of the Castle had a broad and strongly supported roof of canvas, planks, and thatch of rice-stalks; and rooms separated by boards with shelves for storage, and home-made furniture

In order to watch the sea for a ship which might bring about the end of his imprisonment, Crusoe devised a ladder up to the top of the cliff through which his underground suite ran. This was his lookout post, with a wide view of that quarter of the island, its shore and the sea; from here he had observed the arrival of the savages' boats and their devilish sport upon the shore whence he rescued Friday. From this hidden vantage he saw with his telescope the English ship – of which I was captain, but deposed by vicious mutineers – and watched the boatful of ruffians bringing me and my two loyal companions ashore, either to kill us or to abandon us (with little to choose, in our eyes, between these terrible fates). He waited until most of our captors dispersed to explore, the rest asleep in the heat of the afternoon, and stepped from the concealing woods to make himself known to us: an outlandish figure clad in goatskin garments like a latter-day John the Baptist; but unlike the saint in that he bristled with arms, having a pistol, a cutlass, and a musket across each shoulder. I

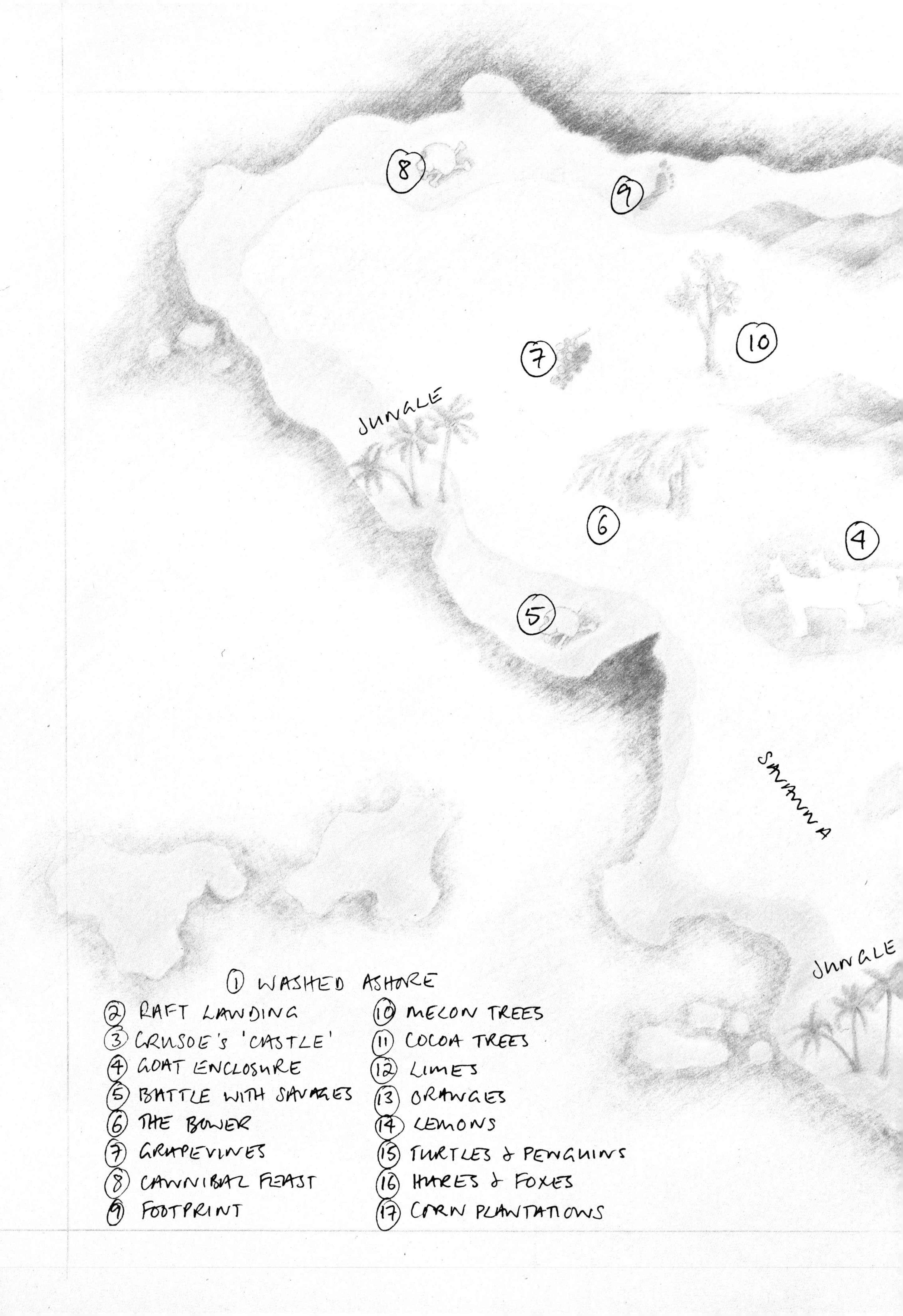
8
9
10
7
JUNGLE
6
4
5
SAVANNA
JUNGLE
1 WASHED ASHORE
2 RAFT LANDING
3 CRUSOE'S 'CASTLE'
4 GOAT ENCLOSURE
5 BATTLE WITH SAVAGES
6 THE BOWER
7 GRAPEVINES
8 CANNIBAL FEAST
9 FOOTPRINT
10 MELON TREES
11 COCOA TREES
12 LIMES
13 ORANGES
14 LEMONS
15 TURTLES & PENGUINS
16 HARES & FOXES
17 CORN PLANTATIONS

15
12
13
14
16
17
3
N
W
E
2
1
S

told him briefly of our plight, and he took us to his castle.

Thus our fortunes changed in an instant, and gratefully we swore to obey him, and follow his plans: for this was only a beginning, and we still had the whole ship's company (some loyal but afraid), as well as the ruffians on the island, to overcome – our greatest fear being that they might yet sail away and leave us helpless. The ingenuity and cunning our new leader showed in waiting for the dark, in dividing and conquering our enemy and adding the waverers to our own band, was masterly. His strategems worked, and when we had secured the ring-leaders in a cave under Friday's guard, we set off in their boat to recapture my ship – where we rushed those on deck, battened down the hatches on the company below, and shot the self-styled "captain" himself, the instigator, in the round-house. It only remained to offer amnesty to the fearful; the remaining ringleaders were given the choice of Justice in England or the confines of Crusoe's island, and gratefully chose the latter.

Now I had leisure to see his little kingdom, especially the fertile vale where he had established his "country house" or "bower", with its flourishing grain, its grapevines heavy with fruit, its pens of goats. This flock, with the birds he shot and the turtles he found on the shore, had been his provender; supplemented by bread from his own corn, and washed down with goats' milk or coconut milk. All this, together with his castle, his bower, his boat (knowing full well no escape could be made in it), he now bequeathed to the mutineers; and he, with the trusty Friday, sailed with us. He had indeed made his prison a home – but looked his last upon it with deepest thankfulness, and returned to the world of men.

ALICE'S ADVENTURES IN WONDERLAND

"'Would you tell me, please, which way I ought to go from here?'

"'That depends a good deal on where you want to get to,' said the cat.

"'I don't much care where —' said Alice.

"'Then it doesn't matter which way you go,' said the cat.

"'— so long as I get somewhere,' Alice added as an explanation."

It was Alice who told me how to get there. After tea – she remembered, as always, to set down a saucer of milk for me – we went into the nursery, and I settled in her lap. Alice knows just how to scratch behind my ears, and how to stroke me gently under my chin, and I never mind if she likes to talk at the same time.

On that day she wanted to tell me about her strange adventures which had started when she had seen a white rabbit wearing a waistcoat and consulting a pocket watch. Nearly as curious as a cat, Alice decided to follow him, and she tumbled down a rabbit-hole into a very peculiar place indeed.

"Oh, Dinah, I wish you had been with me," she said. "For it was all very strange, and I would never have felt lonely if you had been with me. And then you would have enjoyed meeting all those odd creatures, I'm certain. There was a mouse with a very long tail . . . and all those birds . . . although perhaps they wouldn't have been so friendly to *you* as they were to me. Isn't it curious that cats should like birds so much, and birds not like cats? I never before thought to wonder, but what if the puddings that I like so much don't like me?"

I purred, meaning: continue stroking. Usually Alice understands, but that time she didn't, and said: "Now, what do you mean by that? The trouble with your language is that it all

sounds the same, no matter what you mean. If only you could speak properly! You know, I'm certain that if you had gone with me you would have been able to speak. All the other animals could."

Then she gave me a little shake and said, "Why, I believe you could speak to me now, if you only put your mind to it. After all, you're very intelligent – you always understand everything I say, and you have the most expressive voice. I'm sure you're only pretending you can't speak, you provoking creature!" And she shook me again, slightly harder. I didn't like that, so I wriggled out of her grasp and ran away, and heard no more about it just then.

But I didn't forget what she had told me, and I wanted to see Wonderland for myself. The very next day, instead of hiding in a bush to wait for birds, or hunting mice in the hay, I went directly to the field and found the rabbit hole.

Usually I don't have anything to do with rabbits, and I would never dream of squeezing myself into a dark, narrow rabbit hole, but I had

heard where this one led. And, sure enough, no sooner had I entered before I was falling gently and slowly down – so gently it was almost like floating, and I wasn't at all afraid. Still, it was a relief to land safely on my own four feet at the bottom.

I found myself in the hall Alice had told me about: there were all the locked doors, and there the glass table with the golden key, and even the bottle labelled "Drink Me." I sniffed: cherry tart, custard, pineapple, roast turkey, toffee and hot buttered toast mingled, just as she had said. I was careful not to put out my tongue in case even a drop should shrink me. I could see some advantage to being larger, but if I was any smaller I might find myself being chased by a mouse, and that wouldn't do at all!

Making my way out of the hall I found myself

in a wood, and there, in a clearing, stood the little house which belonged to the Duchess. There was a fish in front dressed up as a footman (in spite of having no feet) and a pig dressed as a baby, and remembering that Alice had told me the house was full of loud noises, pepper, and flying crockery, I decided not to go in.

I was hoping to find the Cheshire Cat. Alice had told me of his ability to fade in and out of sight, and that sometimes only his grin could be seen. If I met him, perhaps he would teach me the trick. What a stir that would cause at home, I thought. I'd love to tease the dog next-door,

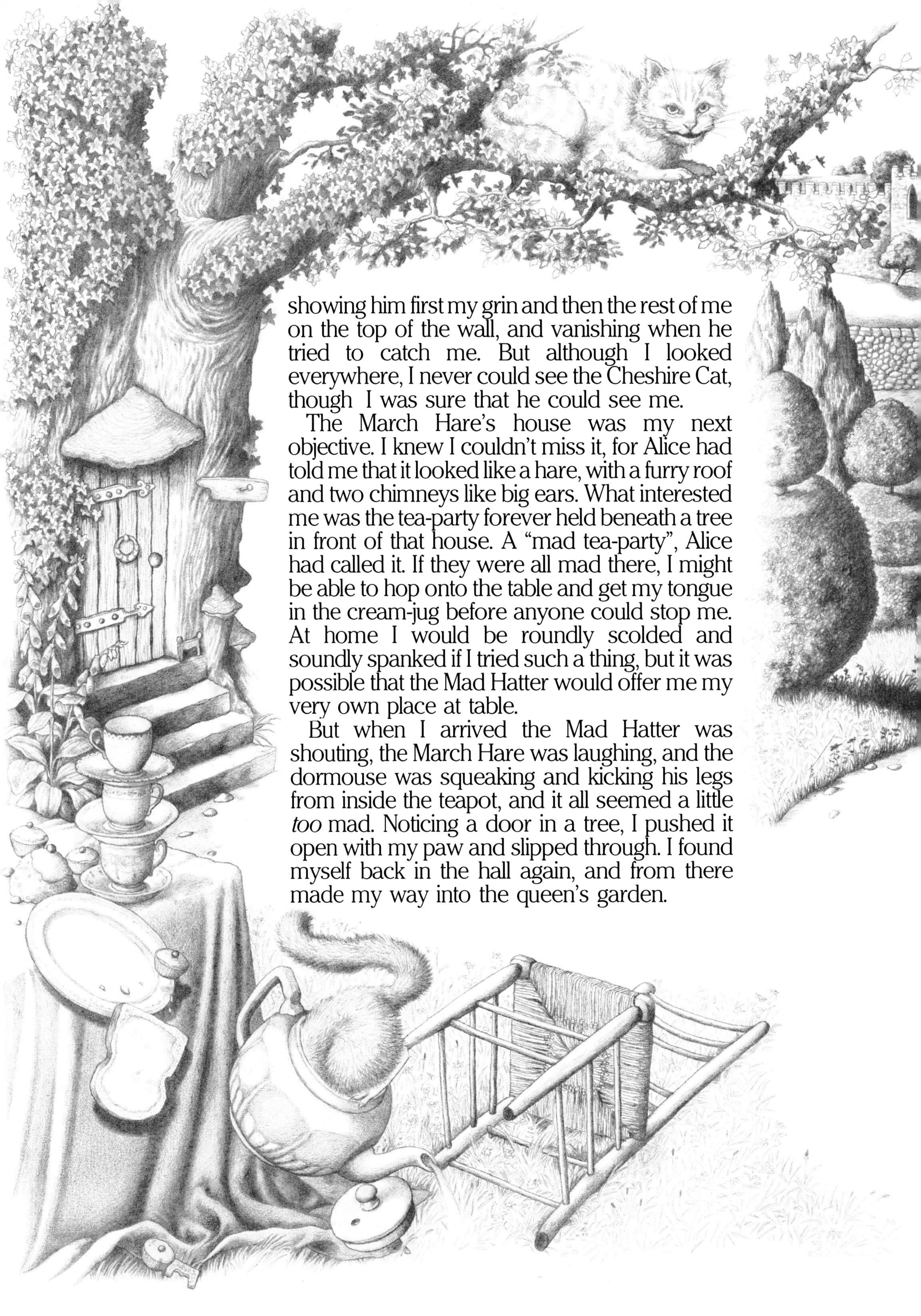

showing him first my grin and then the rest of me on the top of the wall, and vanishing when he tried to catch me. But although I looked everywhere, I never could see the Cheshire Cat, though I was sure that he could see me.

The March Hare's house was my next objective. I knew I couldn't miss it, for Alice had told me that it looked like a hare, with a furry roof and two chimneys like big ears. What interested me was the tea-party forever held beneath a tree in front of that house. A "mad tea-party", Alice had called it. If they were all mad there, I might be able to hop onto the table and get my tongue in the cream-jug before anyone could stop me. At home I would be roundly scolded and soundly spanked if I tried such a thing, but it was possible that the Mad Hatter would offer me my very own place at table.

But when I arrived the Mad Hatter was shouting, the March Hare was laughing, and the dormouse was squeaking and kicking his legs from inside the teapot, and it all seemed a little *too* mad. Noticing a door in a tree, I pushed it open with my paw and slipped through. I found myself back in the hall again, and from there made my way into the queen's garden.

A cat may look at a king – so Alice tells me – so I wanted my chance. But a stranger lot of royalty can never have been seen by any other cat!

Scarcely able to believe my eyes I watched the Queen and King of Hearts playing an outlandish game of croquet, using flamingos for mallets, hedgehogs for balls, and with soldiers bending over to make themselves living arches. It was all so confusing that I hardly knew what was happening, or how it changed, but I found myself inside a courtroom, and the Queen of Hearts was shouting "Off with his head! Off with her head!" every time she was displeased, which was often.

The white rabbit, the Mad Hatter, and all the people I had seen playing croquet were in the court, but I couldn't make out what the trial was about. I noticed that the jury box was full of an

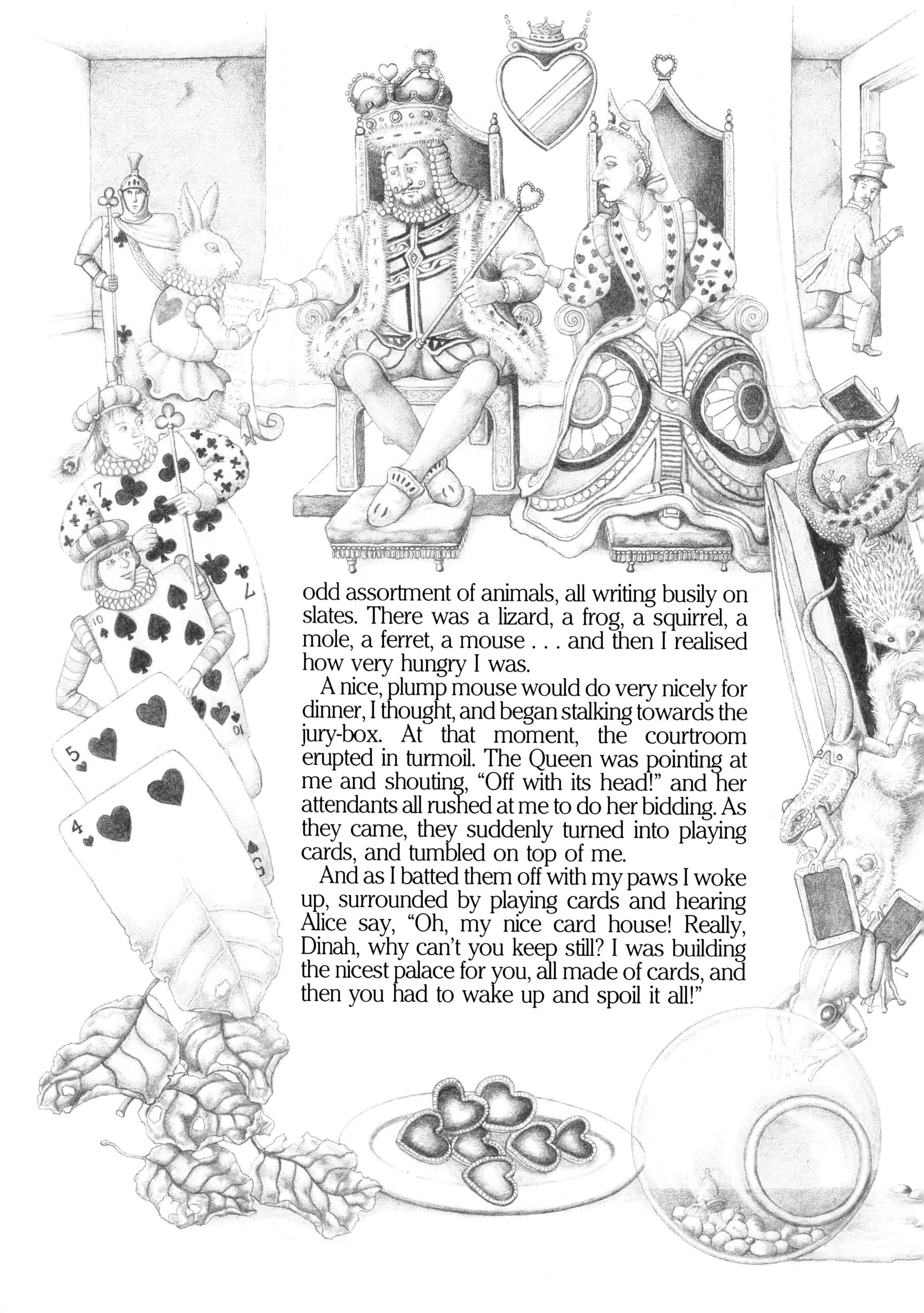

odd assortment of animals, all writing busily on slates. There was a lizard, a frog, a squirrel, a mole, a ferret, a mouse . . . and then I realised how very hungry I was.

A nice, plump mouse would do very nicely for dinner, I thought, and began stalking towards the jury-box. At that moment, the courtroom erupted in turmoil. The Queen was pointing at me and shouting, "Off with its head!" and her attendants all rushed at me to do her bidding. As they came, they suddenly turned into playing cards, and tumbled on top of me.

And as I batted them off with my paws I woke up, surrounded by playing cards and hearing Alice say, "Oh, my nice card house! Really, Dinah, why can't you keep still? I was building the nicest palace for you, all made of cards, and then you had to wake up and spoil it all!"